How to solve 90% of your problems!

Victor Gomes Konecsni

Acknowledgements

I want to thank God for giving me the physical and mental health to reach where I am at this moment.

I am immensely grateful to my wife, who is always by my side, supporting me, giving tips, advising me, correcting my mistakes, but mainly believing in me, even when I have some different ideas, like writing this book.

To my family, who provided me with both financial and moral support, allowing me to learn from life and from the academic world, and for all the support I have always received from them as well.

Contents

Introduction

My name is Victor, I am a psychologist and a specialist in Cognitive Behavioral Therapy (CBT), passionate about the profession for over 10 years. Throughout my life, I have always sought ways to better understand human behavior and thinking. I was fascinated by why one person acts in a certain way and not another, and also by the fact that one person suffers from a situation while another, going through the same situation, does not show any suffering. Was that person really not suffering? Or were they pretending? Or had they learned a way to deal with the situation that didn't make them feel bad? I wanted to discover why a situation affected person X and did not affect person Y.

After graduating in psychology, I remained fascinated by the workings of the human mind. I continued studying, looking for courses, reading books, until I discovered the Cognitive Behavioral Therapy (CBT) approach. I studied human behavior, habits, problem-solving, among other topics. I read several books, watched videos of other psychologists and psychiatrists, always seeking to understand more about human beings.

I specialized in Cognitive Behavioral Therapy at PUCRS (Here in Brazil) and continue to study, seeking to learn the best ways to help solve my patients' issues. Throughout my years in clinical practice, I have treated various patients with different demands, working on issues such as anxiety, depression, stress, insomnia, procrastination, self-awareness, and others like Bipolar Disorder, Borderline Personality Disorder, and Attention Deficit Hyperactivity Disorder (ADHD).

Despite each of these conditions being different in many aspects, such as life experience and the way each person feels the impact of a particular situation, I realized that, at the core, many problems can be solved in similar ways. Of course, there is no magic formula to solve all problems; if there were, it would be easy, and we wouldn't need psychologists, psychiatrists, and other professionals. However, my goal with this book is to make it possible to solve most of your problems. It may seem audacious to say that it is possible to solve 90% of your problems, but what I am proposing is not a magic formula or just a simple strategy, but techniques and tools used in clinical practice that will guide you in dealing with everyday issues that have been bothering you and enable you to become the author of your own story. Or, as we often say in Cognitive Behavioral Therapy, so that you can become your own therapist.

It is worth remembering that this book does not replace seeking a professional, whether a psychologist, psychiatrist, or another specialist who can handle mental health, especially if you are experiencing a high level of suffering. Nowadays, we can find practically everything on Google. It is very easy to have a symptom and search for what you are feeling, and Google will give you various answers and possible treatments, whether for physical or emotional pain. The problem is that this gives a false impression that you can solve and find answers to everything by searching the Internet. But when you are genuinely suffering, there is nothing that will help you in an "automatic" way, and that is why it is important to seek a professional.

With this book, you can work on self-awareness and life development to learn how to better deal with everyday challenges, using techniques and tools in a practical way to increasingly internalize the concepts and thus create new habits that will be healthy for both your mental and physical health.

What is Cognitive Behavioral Therapy (CBT)?

CBT is an evidence-based approach, grounded in scientific studies and research that prove its effectiveness. Developed by Aaron Beck in the 1960s in the United States, this approach works with the concept that our thoughts and the way we perceive and deal with situations directly impact how we feel about them. Depending on your worldview and situations, you can feel happy or sad about a particular situation. Therefore, we work to analyze and reframe the thoughts we have in response to situations.

Have you ever stopped to think that most of our problems are created by ourselves? For example, if a friend or acquaintance passes by and you say "Hi," but they don't respond, what might go through your mind? "They are mad or upset with me; I did something they didn't like." But this doesn't necessarily have to be true. They might be distracted, preoccupied with many concerns and problems, or simply didn't hear you. In other words, you became anxious and worried because of your interpretation and thoughts about that situation.

Additionally, it's very common for people to take on others' problems as their own. You might have a family member going through a difficult time, and instead of trying to guide and talk to this person, you might end up feeling obligated to solve what is bothering them. These are just a few examples of how, often, we create our own problems. We need to analyze and reflect on these and other situations and find ways to deal with them healthily.

Therefore, in this book, you will find various examples, situations, and ways to solve most of your problems practically, without generating more stress and discomfort in your life.

Ah..., you might have wondered why this book teaches you to solve 90% of your problems and not 100%. Well, stay until the end of the book, and I'll tell you what those 10% of problems are.

Important Notice!

Both with this book and in psychotherapy itself, we need to understand that it is a two-way street. In other words, it is not enough to just read the book and know the techniques without putting them into practice, because merely understanding the concept is very different from actually experiencing it.

So, make the most of this book: read one chapter at a time, practice the techniques, and repeat as many times as necessary. Some of them are useful for various situations, meaning you will need to apply them multiple times until you can internalize them and turn them into habits.

If needed, make notes in the book itself or have a notebook to write down the key points, techniques, and reminders. You might be wondering: why a notebook and not a phone or computer? Our mind registers information better when we write with paper and pen than through electronic means. For this reason, I always encourage you to actually write and not just leave the information theoretically in your mind.

Now, with this message given, let's move on to the book.

Chapter I

A man who lived for his job

Of course, work is extremely important, and in most cases, unless you were born into wealth or won the lottery, it is necessary to work to support yourself, help your family, and buy things you want and need. Therefore, I can't tell you to quit your job and do only what you like because that would harm you significantly. The problem arises when you live solely for work, going from home to work and from work to home, without any leisure, fun, physical activities, or other important aspects of life.

Let's consider the case of Mr. Antonio (a fictitious name). Mr. Antonio is 40 years old, married, and has two children, a boy and a girl. He works as a teacher, covering three shifts—morning, afternoon, and evening—at an elementary and high school.

His daily routine is as follows: He wakes up at 5:30 AM, takes a shower, has his breakfast (alone, because his wife is still sleeping), then gets ready to leave, grabs his lunchbox, and drives to work. He arrives at work around 6:30 AM and needs to prepare for his classes. After a tiring morning, he finishes at around 12:00 PM and has lunch. In the afternoon, he starts at 1:00 PM and teaches until 6:00 PM with little time for breaks. Finally, the last shift is from 7:00 PM to 10:00 PM. After this stressful and exhausting day, he goes straight home, has dinner, chats a bit with his wife and children, and needs to sleep to start the next day.

On weekends, he almost never has time for anything because he needs to continue working at home, grading tests, preparing lessons, and handling administrative tasks such as tracking attendance, among other things.

In other words, Mr. Antonio's life is basically work and home, and this is causing many problems in his personal life, in his relationship with his wife and children, and in his physical health. He has no time to do physical activities, no time to schedule appointments to check on his health; in the end, he has no time for anything. It reached a point where Mr. Antonio no longer knew what to do. His life was in chaos, he felt completely lost, and didn't know how to improve. He started experiencing a lot of stress, anxiety, depression, and symptoms like headaches and a racing heart.

Until one day, he decided to seek help because he couldn't stand feeling that way anymore. He sought out a psychologist to find a solution. He had to take some time out of his Saturday for an online session with a psychologist since he never had time during the week. After telling the psychologist everything he was going through, the professional advised him that he needed to reorganize his life because he was overloading only one area and not living the others. Mr. Antonio was confused; he didn't know how he could do this since he had no time for anything. The psychologist then explained that there is a tool called the **Wheel of Life** that could help with this organization.

Wheel of Life

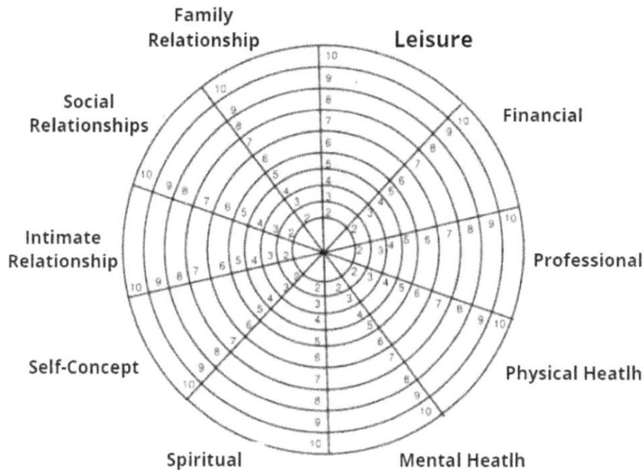

So, the psychologist explained to him:

— You are going to fill out this wheel, rating each area from 1 to 10, with 1 being the lowest and 10 being the highest, based on how you are feeling at this moment.

Mr. Antonio downloaded the exercise and began to reflect on the different areas of his life. He had never thought about this before; he lived his life so automatically, as billions of people do, and had never stopped to reflect on how his life was going. He just knew it was terrible.

After reflecting and starting to fill out the Wheel of Life, he paused to see how the different areas of his life were and was shocked by the results. Most of the scores were extremely low:

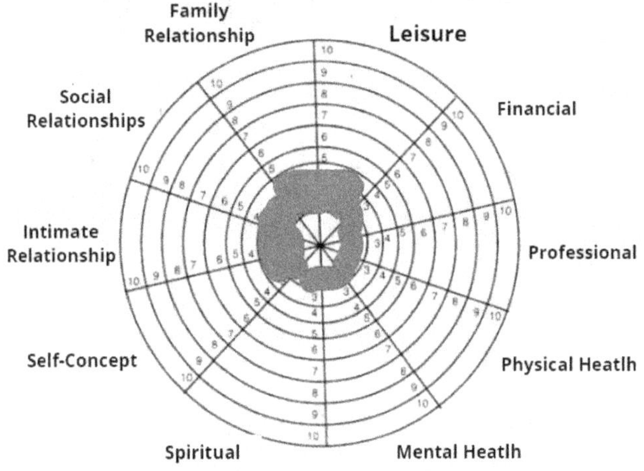

He was shocked and didn't know how he had let his life reach this state. Even though he knew his life had many problems, he hadn't realized how unbalanced it was. After the initial shock, he thought, "Well, the psychologist said to write down the reasons for giving these ratings and also to think of goals to improve my life!"

So he began to write:

Leisure, score 4: It's been years since I've known what it's like to take a vacation, I hardly ever go out to do things I enjoy, like going for walks, going to the beach, going to see movies at the cinema. At most, sometimes on weekends I watch a movie at home, but I miss going to the park, for example. I don't even remember what those things are anymore because work consumes me so much.

Goals: Try to take some time to do activities I enjoy, go out occasionally with my family to the mall, try to go to the park at least once every 15 days.

Financial, score 3: Despite working hard, I don't earn much, and expenses go towards household items, bills, medications, children's clothes. There's hardly anything left, and despite not being in need, I don't have money to buy something nice that I like, or even to travel and go out more often.

Goals: Try to earn more money, see if I can manage my finances better, try to cut some unnecessary expenses, and perhaps create a spreadsheet to track income and expenses.

Professional, score 2: I feel extremely overwhelmed, I practically live for work, spending the whole day at school teaching, then I still need to bring work home and spend hours working on weekends. This makes me very stressed, anxious, and depressed. I want to be able to live, do other things that I enjoy, and have more time for myself and to dedicate to my family.

Goals: Perhaps change jobs, look for another one that pays more, reduce working hours, not overload myself so much, not take on responsibilities that I won't be able to handle and that will harm me.

Physical Health, score 2: It's been a long time since I've been to the doctor; I don't know how my health is. I feel very tired, my heart races often, and there are times I worry I might have a heart attack. I'm very concerned about my health, but at the same time, I don't get tests done. My diet isn't the best; I often end up eating junk food due to lack of time for better meals, or sometimes I even forget to bring my lunch to work.

I haven't exercised in a long time, and it's definitely harming me. I don't have time for the gym or to play any sports.

Goals: Try to find some time to engage in physical activity, but I still don't know how. Try to schedule a doctor's appointment and undergo some health tests.

Mental Health, score 2: I live with stress, anxiety, maybe even panic. Sometimes I don't want to leave the house; I just want to stay locked at home without having to go to work or see other people.

Goals: Continue with therapy consistently, try to improve areas of my life, practice breathing exercises, meditation, and try not to overload myself.

Spiritual, score 2: There was a time in my life when I enjoyed meditation, yoga, and even going to church, but it's been years since I've practiced these. I didn't give a zero because sometimes when I commute to work, I try to use a mantra, but often forget.

Goals: Try to go to church occasionally, or at least practice meditation, set aside time to connect with my spiritual side.

Self-Concept, score 2: I consider myself hardworking, proactive, I try to do things as best as possible, I like helping others, so I consider myself a good person. But at the same time, sometimes I end up being taken advantage of and helping too much. Lately, I don't consider myself a good husband and father because I don't have time for my family.

Goals: Try to find more balance, not to harm myself when helping others, try to dedicate more time to my family.

Intimate Relationship, score 3: I love my wife very much, but it's been a while since we went out together or did any activities we enjoy. Once again, this is because of work. Often, we argue because I bring work home and don't have time for her and the children. This upsets me a lot because I want to do more things with her, go out, take walks, etc.

Goals: Try to set aside some alone time for us to do something together, watch a movie, go out, so we can talk more as well.

Social Relationships, score 3: I have a few friendships that I hardly see. Most of my friendships are from work, and I get along well with them, but it doesn't go beyond that because I don't have time to do anything outside of work. When a friend invites me to go out, I end up having to decline.

Goals: Try to communicate more with friends and set aside time to send messages, try to schedule outings, visit their homes, or at least invite some friends over to my place.

Family Relationship, score 4: My family consists of my wife and children because I no longer have my parents and don't have contact with other relatives like uncles, cousins, etc. I am an only child. I love my wife and children, but the lack of time to spend quality time with them, even at home, really affects me.

Goals: Resolve this issue of time to spend more time with my family, go out more with them, spend more time and engage in activities that connect me with them.

Thus we conclude the Wheel of Life activity. You might be wondering, "Okay, but what now?" Now we need to start putting things into practice. Of course, writing is easier than actually doing, but the most important step is becoming aware of what needs to be changed. After that, there are strategies that can be used to implement these goals and begin improving the areas of life. In the next chapter, I will discuss how to start changing your life in effective ways.

Chapter II

Microsteps

One of the big mistakes people make, especially when they want to start something or when they are having difficulty doing something, is wanting to take big steps. For example, if you start taking a cooking course but have no experience, and in the first class, you want to make an extremely complex recipe, the chances of it going wrong are very high. You don't have the preparation, you don't have the basics, you don't know that before making that recipe, you need to learn how to fry a steak properly, that you need to learn how yeast works to make a more elaborate dessert.

Or let's suppose that you haven't exercised for a long time, and you think: "Starting tomorrow, I will go to the gym every day and train for 2 hours!" The chances of this actually working are very small. In some cases, you might even manage to go for a few days, but soon you will become discouraged because it becomes too overwhelming.

Now, if instead, you say: "I will start gradually, I will do an exercise at home, a 15-minute walk, 3 days a week," it becomes much better. You are starting slowly, getting your body and mind used to it, and after a while, you can increase the quantity and intensity of the exercises.

Therefore, you need to start gradually, through the so-called Microsteps. There are ways for you to start something slowly until you feel secure, confident, and accustomed, turning those activities into habits. When we don't use Microsteps and try to do various things at the same time, or try to take too big steps and can't achieve them, we feel frustrated because what you expected to achieve didn't turn out as you imagined.

And that's how Mr. Antonio started. First, he took the results of his Wheel of Life activity to the psychologist, and after the psychologist's analysis, they began working on the most important points in Mr. Antonio's life areas.

The psychologist:

- Analyzing your responses from the Wheel of Life, I see that what is most negatively impacting all areas right now is the professional part, which is even rated a 2. Now, how do you think you could start working to improve this area, considering Microsteps?

Mr. Antonio:

- Well, since I can't just quit or change jobs overnight, I need to think about what I can do right now. The first thing I can do is stop doing activities that aren't my responsibility. Instead of always trying to help others, I need to think about my well-being and my family's well-being. So, I will start by fulfilling only my duties to have a bit more free time. Additionally, I will start talking to other people, friends, acquaintances, and even send resumes to other schools to see if I can find another job.

The psychologist:

- Perfect, these actions will already help you start to have some direction and gradually work in this area. Next week, tell me how it went.

Mr. Antonio:

- Agreed!

The following week, Mr. Antonio returns excited to the session, reporting what he has already managed to do.

Mr. Antonio:

- This week has been liberating. Even though I am using Microsteps and understanding that everything I am doing is part of a process, I have already started to see some excellent results. I started doing only what is my responsibility, and this has already freed up a bit more time during the week and also on the weekend! I can't wait to see what the next steps will be.

With these initial steps, Mr. Antonio managed to start getting his life back on track. First, he was able to free up some time in his schedule both during the week and on weekends, giving him more time for his family and other activities. After a few weeks, he secured a better-paying job at another school in the afternoon shift. He began working only in the morning and afternoon, freeing up his evenings for other activities and spending more time with his family.

He started taking care of his health, finding time for leisure, being more with his family and friends, and feeling less stressed and overwhelmed. He realized that life isn't just about work and that he can indeed have a balance in different areas of his life. By using Microsteps, he began making small changes in his daily routine and noticed gradual improvements, leading to significant enhancements over time.

After six months, the psychologist asked Mr. Antonio to do the Wheel of Life again, and this was the result:

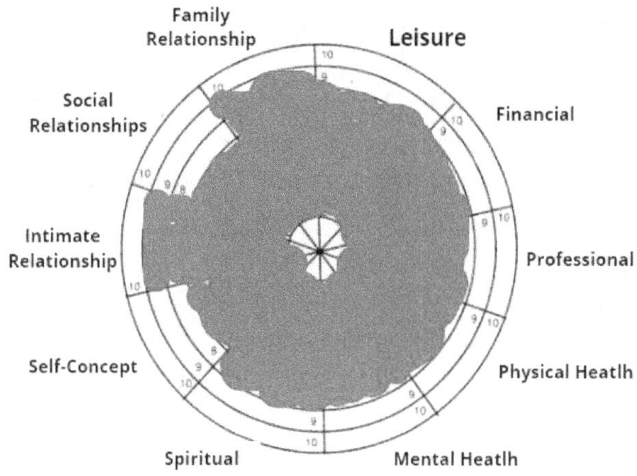

In Mr. Antonio's case, since the biggest problem was work, resolving this issue helped him address most other areas of his life:

Leisure, score 8: Now I have time to go out, travel, and even practice some hobbies that I never thought possible before, like playing the guitar. Besides, I can now go to the park, cinema, and more. I started by organizing my schedule and researching places I wanted to visit on the Internet. First, I explored my city, made a list of outings and hobbies I wanted to pursue, and gradually started doing them, increasing the number of activities over time.

Goals: Continue to make time for leisure, both alone and with family, and travel more.

Financial, score 8: Despite working less, I am now earning more because I changed jobs. I can manage my finances better, created an Excel spreadsheet, and am controlling my spending, avoiding unnecessary expenses like I used to. First, I made a list of my monthly expenses and identified what I could cut. I canceled unused streaming subscriptions and reduced takeout orders, among other things.

Goals: Maintain this financial standard and perhaps, in the future, find ways to earn more money while working less. I'm considering giving private lessons as well.

Professional, score 8: One of the "turning points" was starting to use microsteps. I made a list of places to send my resume and people I could ask for help in finding another job. Additionally, I only do what is within my responsibilities, still considering myself a dedicated professional. I no longer take a lot of work home or work on weekends, which gives me much more free time and makes me feel much better.

Goals: Continue to strive to be a quality professional while always remembering to prioritize myself.

Physical Health, score 8: My health is very good. I went to the doctor, did the necessary tests, and despite some issues like high cholesterol and elevated blood pressure during stressful moments, I improved my diet and practiced physical activities using the microsteps technique. I started slowly, doing a 15-minute home exercise every other day, then gradually increased it. I began walking near my house, then at the park, until my body got used to it, and I started going to the gym. Now it's a habit, and I even feel uncomfortable if I don't go to the gym.

Goals: Maybe try a different activity. I really want to swim and buy a bike to ride occasionally.

Mental Health, score 8: I can't say I'm 100% yet. I still experience stress daily, including at work, but situations affect me much less, thanks to therapy and my own efforts. I now manage conflicts better. Situations that would have caused significant stress before are much calmer now.

Goals: At the moment, just maintain what I'm already practicing and continue using the techniques I've learned.

Spiritual, score 8: Now I can attend church more frequently, which gives me peace, especially going with my family. I'm practicing yoga and have even visited some Buddhist temples, breathing and meditation help me a lot.

Goals: Continue as I am.

Self-concept, score 7: I know I can still improve as a person, father, and husband, but at the same time, I'm happy to be evolving every day. I keep striving to dedicate myself to my family, friends, and as a human being.

Goals: None at the moment.

Intimate Relationship, score 9: I give it a 9 because I believe there's always room for improvement, but everything is wonderful. Now I have more time to spend with my wife. We can talk, watch movies together, go out, and visit places we like. We now share hobbies, go dancing, and attend shows we enjoy, which we never had time for before.

Goals: Renew our wedding vows.

Social Relationship, score 7: There's still room for improvement, but I can now arrange to visit friends or have them over. I started by sending messages, replying more promptly. My friends are now more hopeful about inviting me out. Whenever possible, I arrange something with them or at least make a video call if I can't meet in person.

Goals: Maybe plan a trip with some friends, rent an Airbnb at the beach or another cool place.

Family Relationship, score 9: My relationship with them is great now. We relate much better. I have time to watch my children grow, attend their school events, and parent-teacher meetings that my wife used to attend alone. I truly feel like a present father now.

Goals: None at the moment.

In the end, what Mr. Antonio needed was to gain a perception of how the areas of his life were and what he could do to improve them. Often, what we lack is awareness of a particular situation so that we can change it.

As we also noticed, Mr. Antonio used the microsteps technique to gradually improve the areas of his life without generating frustration from trying to do everything at once and failing.

And you? Have you stopped to think about how the areas of your life are?

Below, I will leave a blank Wheel of Life exercise for you to fill out. You can complete it on this page, or if you prefer, you can fill it out separately with paper and pen, or create a file on your computer or phone.

Family Relationship
Leisure
Social Relationships
Financial
Intimate Relationship
Professional
Self-Concept
Physical Heatlh
Spiritual
Mental Heatlh

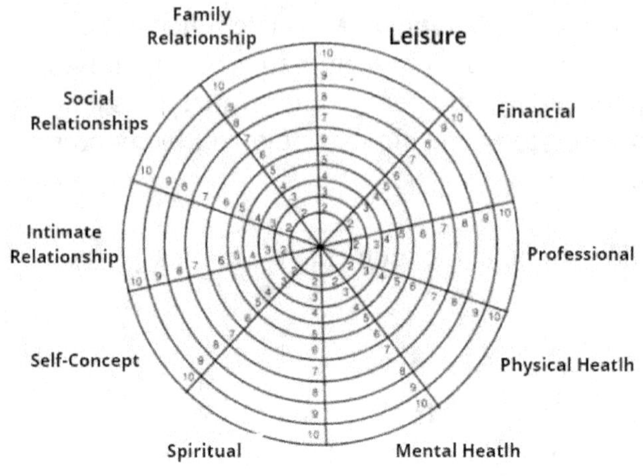

Leisure:

____
____
____
____
____
____
____
____
____
____
____

Goals:

Finantial:

Goals:

Professional:

Goals:

Physical Health:

Goals:

____

____

____

____

____

Mental Health:

____

____

____

____

____

____

____

____

____

____

____

____

____

____

____

____

____

Goals:

____

Spiritual:

Goals:

____

____

____

Self concept:

____

____

____

____

____

____

____

____

____

____

____

____

____

___

Goals:

____

____

____

____

____

Intimate relationship:

____

____

____

____

____

____

____

____

____

____

____

____

____

____

____

Goals:

____

____

____

____

____

Social Relationship:

Goals:

Family Relationship:

____
____
____
____
____
____
____
____
____
____
____
____
____
____

Goals:

____
____
____
____
____

Chapter III

Building Habits

There are many studies about what is necessary for habit formation and how long it takes for a type of activity or behavior to become a habit. Some studies say it takes 21 days, others 26 days, but this depends on various factors such as consistency and the intensity of the practice. As we saw in the previous chapter, if you want to start something that you find difficult abruptly and are not prepared for it, you may end up frustrated by not being able to create the habit you desire.

Let's suppose you want to create the habit of studying, whether for a course you are taking or for a competitive exam you really want to pass. Generally, people think, "I need to study all day," or "I need to study 4 to 6 hours a day," but if you don't have this habit, the chances of success are very low.

Or even if you manage it, you might create a habit known as "flash in the pan," meaning you are super excited about the new activity in the first few days, but after a while, you lose motivation because you didn't have time to really transform it into a habit. Instead, you need to prepare your body and mind to create the habit of studying, for example.

This applies to a range of issues, whether it's the habit of training for a race, learning to play an instrument, or any other type of habit you want to develop.

Let's think about the steps you can follow to
effectively build a habit and ensure that it stays
with you.

Aline (a fictitious name), 26 years old and currently
unemployed, was studying for a competitive exam
in the field of law, in which she had graduated.
However, she had great difficulty staying focused.
She had bought a preparatory course for the exam,
and in it, the teachers said:

"- If you don't study for 6 hours a day and give up
your social life, forget having fun, and enjoying
your leisure time, you won't pass."

Of course, when she heard this, she became very
worried and upset because she wasn't used to such
an intense routine. Despite being a dedicated
person, she couldn't study for such long hours. She
enjoyed going out with friends, having fun,
watching series, and other activities.

The first few days of her attempt at intensive
studying were frustrating. She tried to study for
hours, but it resulted in exhaustion, sadness, and
feelings of incompetence. She began to feel very
anxious and sad because she could only manage to
study for an hour at a stretch. After that, she would
get tired, and the content wouldn't sink in anymore.
She wanted to do something else and would end up
distracted, falling into the well-known trap of

procrastination. She would pick up her phone, scroll through social media, watch videos to distract herself, and before she knew it, hours had passed while she was "resting," and she couldn't get back to studying. At the end of the day, she felt very sad and frustrated because she hadn't studied as much as she wanted. She then began searching the internet for study techniques, found several, but couldn't implement them. She would try them, manage for a while, and then stop.

Finally, she decided to seek help from a psychologist. During the session, she explained what was happening, all her difficulties and frustrations, and that she couldn't study and was procrastinating a lot. The psychologist began to guide her and explain what she could change in her daily routine.

Psychologist:

- First, you need to start thinking in terms of microsteps. When we set too many activities to be done throughout the day and can't accomplish them (something that happens very often), it creates frustration. Because of this, you end up watching series or trying to distract yourself to forget that bad feeling. Let's start by creating a routine, but this routine has to be light. You need to gradually get used to it since it's not something you're used to do. So, I'll give you a simple chart that you can use to create a routine. Ideally, you should make this routine on a whiteboard, a poster board, or even on a sheet of paper, because having a visual impact often works better than making notes on the computer or setting alarms on your phone. The chart is as follows:

Hours	Monday	Tuesday	Wednesday	Thursday	Friday
8:00am					
9:00am					
10:00am					
11:00am					
12:00pm					
1:00pm					
2:00pm					
3:00pm					
4:00pm					
5:00pm					

6:00pm					
7:00pm					
8:00pm					

Psychologist:

- So I would like you to fill in by adding some activities that you want to do, you don't need to fill in everything, especially to avoid overloading yourself, but try to add activities gradually, as you feel you're able to complete these tasks you can add more gradually. And try to schedule shorter times, for example, instead of planning to study four hours a day, try to schedule at least 1 hour, or even less if necessary, always thinking in terms of baby steps. As you complete the activities, you can tick them off or cross them out as well, this will give you a sense of "mission accomplished". Additionally, it's important for you to allocate leisure time, so you don't feel bad about taking time to watch series, go for a walk, etc.

Aline then went home and put into practice the table that the psychologist provided, she tried to think about the most important tasks that she couldn't neglect, and if there was time left, she could do other activities, like going out, watching series, doing household chores. After much reflection, she created the following table:

Hours	Monday	Tuesday	Wednesday	Thursday	Friday
8:00am	Gym	Gym	Gym	Gym	Gym
9:00am	Study	Study	Study	Study	Study
10:00am					
11:00am					
12:00pm					
1:00pm	English	English	English	English	English
2:00pm	Study	Study	Study	Study	Study
3:00pm					
4:00pm	Series	Series	Series	Series	Series
5:00pm	Have fun	Have fun	Have fun	Have fun	Have fun

She felt very happy to be able to fit the activities and especially studying into her routine, and also to have something concrete she could use to visualize what she had to do, what had already been done, and this generated a pleasant feeling. However, she was still having difficulties with a very important point that prevented her from doing the activities she wanted, the famous Procrastination.

Why did she still spend hours on social media, watching videos, even though she had set aside specific times for leisure?

She didn't know what to do, so the following week when the day of her appointment with the psychologist arrived, she reported what was happening, and the psychologist began to guide her.

Psychologist:

- Your table looks great; you didn't put too many tasks, you tried to set some schedules for activities, but when we think about procrastination, it involves some important factors, for example. Our brain tends to prefer things that are easier and put aside what is harder, so it is easier to watch a video, browse social networks, than to study, read a book, or do some work, because when we think about these distractions like social networks, we have immediate rewards. For example, you watch a funny video and already laugh at the time, but when you have to study, do a job, the reward will take a while to arrive, you will need a long time to feel satisfied. So one of the most important points we have in this sense is to reverse roles, that is, to make what is easy difficult and to make what is difficult easy.

Let's think about the case of studies and social networks, how could you make it easier for you to stay focused on studies and make it difficult to access social networks?

Aline:

- I can delete social media apps, I've actually done that before, but then I installed them again. Now, about making studying easier, I'm not sure.

Psychologist:

- Perfect, you can either delete the apps or restrict their use. For example, many phones have a function where you can control the amount of time you can spend on a specific app each day. Once that time is up, you can no longer use it. Alternatively, you can download an external app that does this. Additionally, it's good to keep your phone away from you—leave it in another room, hide it—so you're not tempted to pick it up to watch videos or do other things.

Now, about making studying easier, you can start by preparing your environment. If possible, avoid studying in your bedroom because your brain associates it with rest. Even if your bedroom is your only option for studying, avoid studying on the bed because you might feel lazy and want to sleep. Try to create a dedicated study space. For instance, if you have a small desk in your room, remove anything that could distract you and keep only your books and computer for accessing ebooks and platforms needed for studying.

These adjustments will help you focus on studying. Also, try to take short breaks between study sessions—use the restroom, drink water, especially when you feel tired. These small adjustments will increasingly help you develop effective habits because you're taking small steps and making it easier for your body and mind to perform those activities.

So, to develop habits or even change habits, repetition is needed, but we also need the right strategies. That means starting gradually, analyzing what needs to be done to help develop this habit—whether through making it easier or harder, establishing routines—but always aiming to create a solid habit that won't fade after a week.

After putting these strategies into practice, Aline found it much easier to develop the habit of studying. It became increasingly natural and easy for her until she reached the point where she could increase her study hours—first to two, then to three. She chose not to increase further to avoid exhaustion. However, three hours of quality study per day helped her pass the exam she had been aiming for. Even after passing the exam, she continued her study routine, this time not for an exam but to gain more knowledge in her profession. She achieved these results because she was focused, which brings us to another important point in creating habits... Goals, Objectives, and Motivation. But I'll explain more about that in the next chapter.

Chapter IV

Goals, Objectives and Motivation

Bruno (fictional name), 32 years old, single, and living with his parents, wasn't working or studying. He spent most of his time playing games, watching series, and hanging out with friends. He was sociable, had a good number of friends, and a girlfriend named Luana (fictional name). His life seemed fine outwardly, but he was living day by day without motivation, goals, or objectives. He didn't know which path to follow. His parents felt uneasy because he lacked purpose and encouraged him to think about his future and what he wanted to do. Bruno wasn't being defiant; he simply didn't know which direction to take.

So his family decided he needed to seek help from a psychologist to get guidance on what to do. When they proposed this idea to him, he found it interesting and became hopeful. The following week, the day of his session arrived, and he explained to the psychologist what was happening and why he had come to therapy.

Before discussing his experience with psychotherapy, we need to understand the difference between Goals, Objectives, and what Motivation is.

Goal: It's something that comes before the objective, they are steps that allow you to know that you are progressing towards your "final result".

Nowadays, a term also used is Microgoals, which are very small goals that you can establish so that it's not too overwhelming.

Objective: It's where you want to get to, the end of a path, usually something more long-term that requires passing through several stages or goals to achieve it.

Motivation: Motivation is an impulse that makes people act to achieve their goals. It's something that drives you to take action, helping you follow a certain path, knowing that you will reach a specific destination in the end.

Now, to exemplify these three concepts, let's suppose your objective is to lose 20 kg, which is where you want to end up in the end. Then you set goals: going for walks, doing physical exercises, dieting—everything that will help you achieve this objective. However, this can often be challenging, especially if you focus solely on the objective. That's why we need to think about microgoals.

Instead of focusing on losing 20 kg right away, what if you focus on losing 2 kg first, then another 2 kg, until you reach 20 kg? In other words, you would focus on something easier to achieve and consequently feel more motivated each time you realize you are meeting your goals and getting closer to the objective.

Psychologist:

- I understand. Something very important in our lives, even to give us direction and prevent us from feeling lost, is having Goals and Objectives. Knowing where you want to go is the first step because, as the Cheshire Cat from Alice in Wonderland said, "If you don't know where you want to go, any road will take you there."

That's why it's crucial to establish where you want to go in order to create an action plan and think about strategies to get there.

The psychologist then introduced Bruno to the Wheel of Life and an exercise called the Road Map.

The Road Map exercise is quite simple. Basically, you take a sheet of paper and draw a line, envisioning it as a road. First, you identify the most important points from the Wheel of Life and consider what goals and objectives you can set for those areas. How can you improve them, even in the long term?

Then, on the Road Map, you sketch out where you see yourself in 5 years.

Afterward, you will begin to backtrack, for example, what you need to do in the previous years to achieve those goals, then you will build an action plan thinking about how to get where you want to go.

Bruno took the exercises home, did the Wheel of Life, and then thought about what he would like to put on the Road Map, thinking about what would be most important to him, so the activity looked like this:

In 1 year:

- I want to have found a job.
- I want to start college.
- Begin making plans to move out of my parents' house.

In 2 years:

- I want to start saving money.
- I want to be enrolled in an English course.
- Begin looking for a house or apartment to move into.

In 3 years:

- I want to have moved out of my parents' house and be planning to get married.
- Begin saving for a car.

In 4 years:

- Achieve a promotion at work.
- Have bought a car.
- Get married to my girlfriend.

In 5 years:

- Finish college and start working in my field.
- Perhaps consider starting my own business or having an extra source of income.

After filling out the Road Map, Bruno began to get an idea of which path to follow. Of course, he still needed to start implementing his plans, but after this exercise, he felt motivated and realized he wasn't completely lost anymore.

The next steps involved creating an action plan, considering what would be necessary to start down this path and always thinking in terms of small steps. He thought about what he needed to do to put his 1st-year plan into action, so he decided to break down his goals into a step-by-step process:

I want to have found a job:

To achieve this goal, he first needed to find a job. So, he started thinking about the possibilities to achieve this goal:

always remember the progress he is making more and more each day.

Another important point is that now that he has his motivation, goals, and objectives, he needs to be cautious not to compare himself, especially on social media, because this can lead to something known as FOMO, "Fear of Missing Out," which is the feeling of being left behind or that you are lagging behind because others, whether on social media or people close to you, are achieving things and it seems like you are not.

Comparison is one of the worst enemies one can have when on the path to achieving goals and objectives, things like:

- "Oh, but my friend got a job very quickly." Or:
- "I've seen people on social media who are achieving things much faster than me; I'm taking too long to reach my goals."

We need to understand that everyone achieves their goals and objectives at their own pace. It could be that the person you saw on social media started before you and that's why they've already achieved that job, car, house, etc. Or perhaps they received some kind of help; for instance, their parents might have paid for their education or helped them in other ways. There are many possibilities we can't know for sure.

What we do know is that comparing yourself to others will only make you feel frustrated and demotivated. The only comparison you should make is with your past self. For example, if you're learning English and feel like you're progressing slowly, start looking at other aspects. For instance, last week you didn't know a specific word in another language, but this week you do. Or maybe you used to listen to songs in another language without understanding them, but now you grasp them better. Focus on these micro-achievements.

Have you noticed how important "micro" words are? Micro-steps Microgoals, Micro-achievements Yes, because most people forget about these small things and only care about the macro, which is why they feel frustrated. They want everything as quickly as possible, they want everything yesterday, without paying attention to the gradual progress. But if you start paying attention to the micros, you'll have a different perspective on situations and realize you've accomplished more than you thought.

Another very important point that hinders your progress, and consequently your goals and objectives, making you feel unmotivated, is self-criticism. Have you heard of self-criticism? You know when you do something good or important, but you think it's not enough? You feel like you need to do more or hear that famous phrase "You've only done what's expected of you." It's not just others who make these demands; many people impose them on themselves. For instance, you might be studying for a competition, putting in effort and dedication, but then that little voice comes in:

- This isn't enough, you're doing too little.

You take some time to rest or have leisure time and start feeling bad because you should be studying, working, or whatever. This leads to excessive productivity or hyper-productivity, a feeling that you need to be productive all the time and can't rest or have leisure time. Instead of helping, these thoughts harm you, causing you to feel overwhelmed and tired, stressed, and possibly leading to burnout.

All these points, such as self-criticism, hyper-productivity, and even perfectionism, often go hand in hand because they can all relate to a belief of inadequacy (I'll talk more about beliefs later) that you always need to deliver more and more, which never ends.

Of course, there's nothing wrong with wanting to dedicate yourself, striving to give your best in a particular aspect, whether it's work, a test, a relationship. But everything has a limit. How far is it healthy, and how much are these behaviors harming you? For example, you dedicate so much to something that you feel tired, never have time for anything else, and feel that something that usually takes, say, 30 minutes to complete ends up taking 3 hours because you keep redoing it or starting over from scratch.

Now, how do you deal with these issues to stop self-sabotaging?

> You need to become aware of what you're doing. Are you criticizing yourself too much? Do you have perfectionist behaviors?

> Start making a list of what you're doing. Are you taking too long to complete a task, or do you study extensively for an exam, yet always feel like you're doing too little?

> Begin to jot down all the "good" things you've been doing, all the progress you've made. For example:

Last week, I managed to read 10 pages of a book.

I've been waking up half an hour earlier this week, allowing me to exercise.

Start rewarding yourself:

This afternoon, I deserve to watch 2 episodes of my favorite series because this morning I managed to study for an hour.

Writing is very beneficial for our brains. If possible, keep a diary and jot down everything you've done throughout the day. If you notice you've procrastinated a lot during the day, start changing gradually with what we've seen in the previous chapters: micro-steps, techniques to make things easier or harder.

Now, if you find yourself working too much, overburdened, start appreciating and, at the same time, take some time to relax and do an activity you enjoy.

And now, where to go next?

Even after setting goals and objectives, you might still feel a bit lost, unsure which path to take, unsure which choice is best—should I go down path A or path B? And what if I choose one path and regret it?

To know where to go next, the most important thing is to carefully analyze both options. Make a list of the Advantages and Disadvantages of each path. This way, you can see which one makes more sense for you and avoid the feeling of regret for not taking the other path because you will have weighed each option, like balancing scales, and will have concrete information to help you decide between one or the other.

Another excellent way to discover which path you want to take is by trying it out. For example, suppose you're undecided between a job in sales or a job as an English teacher. If you have the opportunity, try one of the paths—provided it doesn't cause you any harm—because it becomes easier for you to know if you like it there or not.

Julio (fictional name), 17 years old, had a lot of doubt about which profession to pursue when starting college. He had no professional experience yet, so he didn't know what to pursue. He took a vocational test that suggested he could work in healthcare, as a psychologist, or as a veterinarian. However, he wasn't sure if he would like these professions, so he started gathering as much information as possible about each one. He searched for videos on the Internet, read articles about each profession, made a list of pros and cons, and leaned towards studying psychology. But at the same time, he loved animals.

After much reflection, he realized he could pursue a career in psychology, but if he didn't like it, he could switch professions. In the meantime, he volunteered at an animal welfare NGO. He eventually found his passion in psychology and continued to help animals in his spare time.

In other words, he reflected deeply on which path to take and ultimately managed to combine his two passions. He could have not identified with psychology and preferred to change his course, and there's no problem with that because sometimes we make certain choices only to realize that it's not the right path. The important thing is to try.

Chapter V

Anxiety and Fear, Villains or Allies? (Emotional Intelligence)

Anxiety is one of the ills of the century, along with stress and depression. Anxiety can harm you in various ways, whether in daily life, specific places like work, studies, or relationships. But is anxiety 100% bad?

To answer this question, we need to understand not only the role of anxiety but also emotions as a whole, hence the term "emotional intelligence."

Emotional intelligence consists of understanding how emotions work and what they are for, because there is no such thing as good emotions and bad emotions as we often hear. Every emotion has a purpose, and most emotions are related to defense mechanisms that our bodies and minds have had for a long time.

I won't talk about all emotions, but I will mention three that are very important: Fear, Joy, and Anxiety.

Fear

Fear has a purpose; it serves to protect you from a potentially dangerous situation. If you are in the jungle and encounter a wild animal, your body will use a defense mechanism by sending blood to your extremities, preparing you to fight or flee, which increases your chances of survival.

Some people believe that fear is something bad, but if you do not have fear in a situation, the consequences can be disastrous. Let's imagine you are going to skydive but do not feel any fear. This indicates that something is wrong because fear should make you feel that "butterflies in your stomach" to prepare for the situation. If you have no fear, you might impulsively jump out of the plane without checking if your parachute is properly secured, which can lead to problems during the jump.

At the same time, if you have excessive fear, you might not be able to leave the house for a job interview or on the day of your first date with someone special you are in love with. The intensity of fear is very important to determine if it is beneficial or harmful. There are cases where fear exceeds the expected level and prevents us from living healthily, leaving us paralyzed by it. When it reaches this extreme, it significantly harms the life of the person experiencing this situation. It is very common for a person to go through a traumatic situation and then start avoiding certain situations.

If a person is mugged on Street X, they may not be able to pass that street again because it has become a traumatic event. This can cause the person to avoid certain important or necessary places, or they may develop fears of specific objects like needles, cars, airplanes, and others.

To deal with these situations healthily, it is important to use a process called Systematic Desensitization, which helps reduce the effectiveness of the fear stimulus. For example, let's imagine that one day you were in a building elevator, and it got stuck, the power went out, or it fell a few floors. After this situation, you might not want to use an elevator again, and just thinking about it makes your heart race, gives you cold sweats, and makes you very nervous. In such cases, you can follow these steps:

Systematic Desensitization

Identify the intensity of the fear: Do you start feeling unwell just by looking at a photo or video of an elevator? Or does it happen when you pass by one?

Gradually expose yourself to the fear: Suppose the trauma is so intense that merely seeing a photo of an elevator triggers responses like tachycardia, tremors, and cold sweats. You can begin to create positive associations with that fear to gradually reduce its intensity.

Get a photo of an elevator; if possible, ask someone to find it for you. Before looking at the photo, close your eyes and take deep breaths until you feel relaxed. Also, imagine a song you like that makes you feel good. Now, open your eyes and look at the photo, noticing how you feel while continuing to listen to the music and breathe. If you start to feel very uncomfortable, close the photo and try again another day.

Increase the levels of exposure: After a while, you'll notice the photo no longer generates those feelings. Start increasing the exposure by watching videos of elevators and repeating the same process. Gradually, you will feel more comfortable until you reach a point where you can approach and even enter an elevator without feeling uncomfortable. At this stage, that traumatic stimulus will no longer have the same impact; it is desensitized.

You can use this practice for various situations that cause paralyzing traumatic fear, such as getting into a car, an airplane, or other similar scenarios.

Joy

Joy is an emotion that makes us feel very good, it drives us, motivates us, and gets us out of bed. It's a pleasurable emotion, and who wouldn't want to feel joyful every day? You might automatically associate joy with a "good" emotion, right? But that's not always the case. Joy can be a wonderful emotion when you have the right context and intensity. For example, if you receive a promotion at your beloved job or find out you're going to be a parent, you may feel great joy depending on the situation.

Now, let's imagine you're at the funeral of a close person and start feeling joyful, laughing, and making jokes. This indicates some imbalance, even if you didn't like the deceased person. This situation shows something is wrong and needs to be investigated. Moreover, if you felt joyful every day, situations would lose meaning. Initially, it might seem wonderful, but soon you would feel very bored. Thus, joy is positive depending on the intensity.

Anxiety

Anxiety is also a defense mechanism that prepares us for something upcoming, something that requires some form of preparation, whether it's an exam you're about to take or a trip you're planning.

It's not necessarily a bad thing. For example, let's say you're anxious about a trip you're really looking forward to. This type of anxiety will help you get ready, schedule the activities you want to do, check if you need to buy any clothes, book the hotel, and other necessary preparations. If you don't have this healthy anxiety, you might leave everything to the last minute, which can be detrimental because you might not be able to book a hotel or buy a plane ticket if they are all sold out.

If you're going to meet someone you like, anxiety will help you prepare, plan where to go, what to do, and ensure you arrive on time. There's nothing wrong with that. However, when anxiety starts to consume you, preventing you from sleeping, making you neglect daily activities, constantly thinking about the source of your anxiety, and leaving you paralyzed, it becomes harmful and needs to be addressed. This can be through therapy, techniques, or even medication, depending on the case. In this chapter, I will explain how you can manage anxiety using various tools to help you handle everyday anxieties and how to deal with more intense anxieties, like anxiety attacks.

It's also important to note that anxiety, like many other emotions, has levels. It can start as mild anxiety in certain situations, making you a little nervous and worried but still able to handle these situations. Then, there are more disruptive anxieties that make it harder for you to, for example, go out somewhere or make a work presentation, but you can still face them with some effort. Finally, there are severe anxieties that truly paralyze you, preventing you from leaving the house or confronting certain situations, such as social anxiety, which might make you prefer staying home in isolation over attending social gatherings like parties.

We also have Generalized Anxiety Disorder (GAD), which is a higher level of anxiety that is not necessarily related to a specific situation. You can feel anxious and worried at a heightened level without any apparent reason. For example, you might be at home alone washing dishes and start feeling great anxiety, becoming restless and uncomfortable. This type of anxiety typically requires psychiatric support and medication to alleviate these sensations, making psychotherapy more effective.

Lucas (a fictitious name), 19 years old, is in his first year of engineering college and works at his father's bakery. He feels very anxious about the future and college and is almost always anxious. He is very restless, has a whirlwind of thoughts, often shakes his leg, experiences palpitations, and has difficulty breathing, especially during anxiety attacks. Additionally, he suffers from insomnia, frequently waking up at night, having trouble falling asleep, and feeling tired during the day, which affects his attention and focus at work and in his studies.

He considered that he might need medication and discussed it with his parents because he suffers greatly from anxiety. However, his parents suggested he first see a psychologist to determine if medication was necessary. They found a psychologist and scheduled a session for that same week because Lucas could no longer bear the constant anxiety.

On the day of the session, Lucas went to the psychologist's office and explained what he was experiencing. He was very agitated, spoke quickly, and sometimes interrupted the psychologist because he was impatient due to his anxiety.

During the session, the psychologist wanted to teach Lucas an important technique, so he explained.

Psychologist:

- I'm going to teach you an emotional regulation technique that helps stabilize various types of emotions and feelings. Whether you're feeling anxious, stressed, distressed, or even sad about a situation, you can use this technique.

5x5x5 Breathing Technique

Psychologist:

- The first technique I'm going to teach you, and I'd like you to practice it here in the session, is a breathing technique called 5x5x5. You'll inhale while counting to 5, then hold your breath and count to 5 again, and finally, exhale while counting to 5. Ideally, you should breathe through your nose and focus on the sensation of the air entering and leaving your body, as this will help shift your focus away from your worries or problems.

You can use this technique especially during moments of anxiety and stress, but it's also important to set aside a moment of your day to practice it, even if it's just for 2 or 3 minutes. Now, I'd like you to do this breathing exercise here in the session for 2 minutes and then tell me how you feel.

The psychologist set a timer for 2 minutes, and Lucas practiced the breathing technique. After the 2 minutes were up, the psychologist asked Lucas how he was feeling.

Lucas:

- Wow, that's cool. I'm feeling more relaxed. It wasn't very easy because sometimes I started thinking about what I need to do later, so I lost focus a few times, but even so, I feel more relaxed.

Psychologist:

- Perfect, that's normal because you're not used to taking this time to stop and relax. You live a lot on autopilot, rushing through the day, so it's normal for it to be difficult to focus on your breathing at first. The important thing is to practice this regularly so your body and mind can get used to this state of relaxation. Over time, this will become a habit, and you'll automatically start feeling this way.

Now, I'm going to teach you a few more emotional regulation techniques. The next one will also be very important.

Muscle Contraction Technique

When we go through moments of anxiety, stress, especially with high intensity, our body resorts to a defense mechanism that causes our muscles to tense up. This often results in pains, whether in the back, neck, shoulders, or even headaches. That's why many people feel "stiff" even without physical exertion. Have you ever experienced this?

Now, what we need to do is reeducate the body. Since muscle tension is a defense mechanism and automatic, your body only knows how to respond in that way to stress or anxiety.

So, when you find yourself in such tense situations, you can contract all the muscles in your body, making them even tenser than they are, and then release and relax them. This way, your body will learn that it doesn't need to stay tense in that moment, and you will gradually feel calmer and more relaxed.

You can do this technique with 10 repetitions: contract the muscles, count to 5, relax, and repeat this process 10 times.

Mindfulness

Have you ever felt like life is on autopilot? You go through your activities, pass through your day, and before you know it, the day is over!

Then comes another day, and another, and another, all seeming to pass before you without you being able to keep up.

We live in a fast-paced world, filled with numerous tasks and distractions, often missing out on the essential aspects of life, sometimes overlooking small yet valuable opportunities. We think we're living life, but in reality, we're just in an automatic mode, merely existing.

With this in mind, I want to introduce you to a technique that has been gaining widespread use called Mindfulness.

Mindfulness consists of a set of practical and scientifically proven techniques that help you focus on the present moment, without letting the past or future affect you. It aims to make your mind more awake and healthy, becoming your ally.

The goal of mindfulness is to break free from this state of unconsciousness and live a life aware of the present moment, your feelings, and sensations.

Our brain is always seeking pleasure and comfort. This means that the fewer conscious decisions you have to make, the less mental energy you will spend, resulting in more comfort for your brain.

Mindfulness will help you recognize when you've switched to "autopilot" and guide you to exit that state.

Initially, it may feel uncomfortable because it's not something you're accustomed to, but as you practice, it becomes transformative.

Although mindfulness is currently in vogue, the practice has been around for thousands of years, extensively used by various monks and sages since ancient times.

What has changed is that humanity now has scientific means to understand how mindfulness benefits the brain. Numerous studies confirm the effectiveness of mindfulness, showing neurochemical changes in the brain that help reduce stress and anxiety levels, and improve focus and concentration.

Benefits of Mindfulness in Your life

1. Empathy and Patience: When you are mindful and present in the moment, you can channel your energy into feeling empathy rather than wasting it on stress and future-focused concerns. Mindfulness allows you to cultivate patience and understanding, fostering deeper connections with others.

2. Emotional Self-Control: Being aware of your emotions and understanding why you feel a certain way is crucial for emotional self-regulation. This process becomes possible only when you are fully present and attentive to the current moment and your inner state. Through mindfulness practice, this awareness gradually expands, empowering you to navigate your emotions more skillfully.

Mindfulness and Productivity

When you're not living in the present moment and find yourself constantly thinking about what you need to do later or tomorrow, or dwelling on past events, your productivity suffers.

With mindfulness, you focus on the here and now, setting aside unnecessary worries and thoughts for the present moment. This enables you to be much more efficient and productive, performing your tasks with clarity whether at home, work, or wherever you may be.

Mindfulness to Enhance Your Focus

Mindfulness techniques empower you to elevate your focus and concentration, leading to improved performance in your tasks and activities.

These mindfulness exercises involve focusing on your environment or on yourself and are easy to learn and practice. They are already utilized by numerous companies and are also employed as therapeutic techniques.

Mindfulness and Therapy

Given that the focus of therapy is the individual's well-being, mindfulness has increasingly been employed to promote the improvement and overall wellness of patients.

Mindfulness can be integrated into various types of therapy, including psychotherapy, to assist in treatment. It helps calm the mind, ease thoughts and worries, and reduce anxiety and stress. Thus, mindfulness serves as an excellent complement to the utilization of other important practices and techniques.

Exercises to Practice Mindfulness Daily

Mindful eating

Nowadays, it is very common for people to eat quickly or while watching something, whether it's a series, a video, and often they don't even realize what they are eating. They don't taste the food and sometimes don't even notice when they finish eating because they are living on autopilot.

So, when you eat something, whether it's breakfast, lunch, or a snack, take your food, but before eating, pay attention to the colors and shapes of the food. Then, take a deep breath and smell the food. Place it on your tongue, experience the texture, taste the flavor, and savor it as much as possible. Chew slowly, enjoying the sensations. After swallowing, notice the remaining taste in your mouth.

This exercise is good for activating your senses, helping you focus, and exercising your perception. In the beginning, it may be difficult. You may notice that you are trying to practice this, but your mind starts to wander, thinking about problems and worries. Then, bring your attention back to the present moment. It's like exercising a muscle at the gym—over time, you will get used to it, and Mindfulness will become a habit.

Pay attention to sounds

Lie down or sit in a comfortable position, and start paying attention to all the sounds around you, whether they are loud or soft. Notice the sounds that your own body makes. Pay attention to the sounds of birds, the wind, everything around you, and then try to distinguish between the sounds. Focus your attention on one specific sound, then shift to another to train your focus and attention. This meditation helps calm the mind and activate the senses.

Take some time for yourself

Often in the hustle and bustle of daily life, we find ourselves worrying about so many things - work, home, car, family, pets - that we forget to take care of ourselves. So, take a seat in a comfortable place or lie down and do something that makes you feel good. Disconnect from your phone, TV, and anything else that might distract you. Read a book, engage in a sport, but always focus on yourself and how you're feeling. Recognize the importance of taking time for yourself.

Mindfulness during shower time

When taking a shower, focus solely on what you're doing. Feel yourself in that moment, feel the water flowing over your body, listen to the sound of the water falling, smell the fragrance of the soap, shampoo, notice the sensation it brings you. Focus your thoughts and notice how they help you unwind, disconnect from the day's problems. The shower should be a moment just for you, a time to relax, without worrying about what you have to do afterward or tomorrow.

Body Scan

Sitting or lying down, slowly and mentally go through all the parts of your body, from your feet to your head or from your head to your feet. Notice the sensations in each part. Sensations of vibration, pulsation, warmth, coolness. The touch of your clothes on your skin. Extend the awareness of your breath to your entire body. Repeat more than once.

This exercise is good to do before sleeping, as it promotes relaxation.

Mindful Walking

Mindful Walking is a practice where you walk with mindfulness and awareness, focusing on each step and your breath. Find a quiet place to walk, preferably outdoors, and begin by taking slow, deliberate steps. Pay attention to the sensation of your feet touching the ground, the movement of your body, and the rhythm of your breath. If your mind wanders, gently bring your focus back to the present moment and continue walking with awareness. This practice can help calm the mind, reduce stress, and increase mindfulness in everyday life.

Feel the weather, observe and listen to the sound of the birds, or any other sound, the sun, and observe what is around you.

Practice Gratitude

Once a day, stop, relax, and start thinking about everything you're grateful for, all the good things that happened that day. Be thankful for even the simplest things, for life itself, for your body, for your family. Reflect on the things in your life that you're grateful for. Often, we go through the day on autopilot or even complaining about things, and doing this exercise will allow you to realize what you have to be thankful for.

Sleep Hygiene

Having a good night's sleep is fundamental to our lives. A night, or even several nights, of poor sleep can bring various drawbacks such as increased stress, anxiety, and difficulty focusing, and it can also impair memory. Moreover, not sleeping well drains your energy, making you feel more tired and worn out, which negatively affects all aspects of life, whether at work, in studies, or in health. Therefore, we need to work towards improving sleep quality.

Lucas wasn't sleeping well; he had difficulty falling asleep and woke up several times during the night. This was a recurring issue, and he couldn't remember the last time he had a good night's sleep. The psychologist then explained to him the Sleep Hygiene technique, which consists of a series of practices to be done before bed to improve sleep quality.

Step 1: Set a Regular Sleep Schedule

Establishing a consistent sleep schedule is crucial. Although it can be challenging due to various factors such as when you get home and evening tasks, especially if they involve others like family or children, this step is extremely important. Going to bed at different times disrupts your biological clock, making it harder for your body to prepare for sleep.

Lucas used to go to bed at 1:00 AM, but it wasn't a fixed time and sometimes he stayed up even later. He usually woke up at 6:00 AM, getting very little and irregular sleep. He stayed up late because he spent time on social media, playing games, and watching series, which, although enjoyable at the moment, made him more anxious and made it harder to sleep. Following the psychologist's advice, Lucas decided to start going to bed at 11:00 PM, allowing him time to unwind after arriving home and then get to sleep.

Step 2: Calm Your Mind

If your mind is very agitated, write down everything that's bothering you—your thoughts, anxieties, and problems. If you're preoccupied with what you need to do the next day, write that down too. Writing is a way to externalize what's on your mind, as if you're taking your thoughts and worries out of your head and putting them on paper. It's important to write them on paper, not on your phone or computer, as electronic devices can agitate your mind. This leads us to the third step.

Step 3: Disconnect from Electronics

Disconnect from electronic devices such as your phone, TV, and computer. These devices agitate your mind due to the blue light they emit and the overwhelming amount of stimuli. Social media, for instance, bombards you with various information and exciting content, leaving your mind more agitated. Thus, using these devices before bed greatly hinders your ability to sleep.

The third step is to disconnect from electronics at least an hour before your designated bedtime. If an hour seems too long, aim for at least half an hour. For Lucas, disconnecting an hour before bed was feasible, so by 10:00 PM, he had put away his phone, and turned off the TV and computer.

Step 4: Engage in Relaxing Activities

Now that you're not using electronic devices, what should you do? Engage in activities that promote relaxation and prepare you for sleep. For instance, practice the 5x5x5 breathing technique, or read a book—provided it's not a heavy, stimulating book like a horror, suspense, or highly technical book such as one on quantum physics. Opt for lighter reads, such as fiction or historical books.

Reading helps divert your focus from problems and worries, inducing relaxation. If possible, drink calming teas; they help you relax and fall asleep more easily.

Step 5: Stay in Bed if You Wake Up at Night

If you wake up in the middle of the night, avoid getting out of bed unless absolutely necessary, such as needing to use the bathroom. Do not check the time, because seeing that it's, for example, 3:00 AM, and realizing you only have two more hours to sleep, will likely increase your anxiety and make it harder to fall back asleep. The ideal approach is to keep your eyes closed and practice the 5x5x5 breathing technique to help your body and mind relax and make it easier to fall back asleep.

Following these practices, Lucas noticed a significant improvement in his sleep quality. He started falling asleep more easily, woke up less frequently during the night, and felt more energetic and focused during the day. His memory improved, and he began to feel less anxious.

Calm Down Technique

"Calm Down" is a relaxation technique that can help reduce stress and anxiety, promoting a sense of calm and tranquility. It's a simple practice that can be done anywhere and at any time:

Accept your anxiety: Acknowledge and accept the presence of anxiety in your life. Instead of trying to deny or suppress it, allow yourself to recognize that it's normal to feel anxiety in certain situations and that it's a common human experience.

Contemplate your surroundings: Take a moment to observe the environment around you. Pay attention to the details, colors, sounds, and textures present. Mindfulness practice can help shift your focus away from anxiety and bring your awareness to the present moment.

Act with your anxiety: Instead of letting anxiety paralyze you, try to take action despite it. Take small actions that are within your reach, even if they seem challenging. This can help break the cycle of worry and allow you to feel more in control of the situation.

Release the air from your lungs: Breathe deeply and exhale slowly. Focus on releasing tension and stress as you exhale. Deep breathing can help calm the nervous system and reduce anxiety symptoms.

Maintain the previous steps: Continue practicing acceptance, contemplation, action, release, and deep breathing as you face anxiety. These steps can be repeated as many times as necessary to help calm the mind and body.

Examine your thoughts: Notice the thoughts that accompany your anxiety. Question their validity and examine whether they are based on facts or unfounded concerns. Self-observation practice can help reduce the intensity of anxious thoughts.

Smile, you did it!: Recognize and celebrate each small achievement along the way. By facing anxiety and following the steps of the "Calm Down" technique, you're building skills to cope with adversity and promote your emotional well-being.

Embrace the future with acceptance: Maintain an attitude of acceptance toward the future, acknowledging that not everything is under your control and that you are capable of handling whatever happens. Cultivate a mindset of resilience

and adaptation, knowing that you can face
challenges with courage and confidence.

Chapter VI

Practices for Well Being

Nowadays, we go through so many stressful situations and often experience emotions we didn't even know existed, such as anxiety and depression. I've heard many accounts like:

"I thought I'd never know what anxiety was; I've always been so calm. But after some situations, I started feeling very anxious and stressed. I used to think it was nonsense, but now I know it's real."

In this chapter, I want to discuss some crucial aspects of handling daily stress and understanding how we function, why we react in certain ways, and how we can live better.

But before anything else, it's important to work on self-knowledge. Do you know why some days you feel more energetic, while other days you feel sad or anxious? Or even within the same day, why you might feel good at one moment and then start feeling stressed?

Pedro (a fictitious name), 34 years old, experienced many of these moments. Sometimes he was stressed, other times he was cheerful. Some days started off well, and other days began with a sense of depression. People around him even called him "bipolar." The truth was that he had significant mood swings but didn't know why. He felt very troubled because sometimes he felt fine and then suddenly felt bad.

When Pedro went to the psychologist, he was
advised on some well-being practices and was
asked to keep an emotional monitoring journal.

Psychologist:
- First, we need to understand what's causing these
mood swings. Did you know that many aspects of
your daily routine can influence how stressed,
depressed, or anxious you feel? Factors such as diet,
sunlight exposure, well-being practices like
physical activities and meditation, and even
hormonal issues need to be considered. For
instance, how are your blood tests looking?

Pedro:
- It's been quite a while since I had any blood tests
done. I think it's been over a year since I last visited
a doctor.

Psychologist:
- I see. It's important to investigate that. Ask your
doctor to order a comprehensive blood test.

Pedro:
- Sure, I'll ask for that.

Psychologist:
- In addition, we need to understand what's causing
these mood fluctuations. So, I'm going to give you
an exercise called emotional monitoring. You can
fill it out based on how you feel throughout the
week. If you're feeling more cheerful or more sad

or stressed, you can mark it using some faces to indicate your mood, and then write down any relevant situations that happened to make you feel that way.

Emotional Monitoring

	Monday	Tuesday	Wednesday	Thursday	Friday	Saturday	Sunday
Morning							
Happy	😄	😄	😄	😄	😄	😄	😄
Neutral	😐	😐	😐	😐	😐	😐	😐
Sad	🙁	🙁	🙁	🙁	🙁	🙁	🙁
Stressed/Anxious	😠	😠	😠	😠	😠	😠	😠
Afternoon							
Happy	😄	😄	😄	😄	😄	😄	😄
Neutral	😐	😐	😐	😐	😐	😐	😐
Sad	🙁	🙁	🙁	🙁	🙁	🙁	🙁
Stressed/Anxious	😠	😠	😠	😠	😠	😠	😠

<table>
<tr><td colspan="8" align="center">Evening</td></tr>
<tr><td>Happy</td><td>😄</td><td>😄</td><td>😄</td><td>😄</td><td>😄</td><td>😄</td><td>😄</td></tr>
<tr><td>Neutral</td><td>😑</td><td>😑</td><td>😑</td><td>😑</td><td>😑</td><td>😑</td><td>😑</td></tr>
<tr><td>Sad</td><td>😞</td><td>😞</td><td>😞</td><td>😞</td><td>😞</td><td>😞</td><td>😞</td></tr>
<tr><td>Stressed/Anxious</td><td>😣</td><td>😣</td><td>😣</td><td>😣</td><td>😣</td><td>😣</td><td>😣</td></tr>
<tr><td colspan="4">Situation</td><td colspan="4">Thoughts</td></tr>
<tr><td colspan="4"></td><td colspan="4"></td></tr>
</table>

"This exercise you can do at home. Mark it with a pencil, or if you prefer, make a copy of this page to fill out. Try to pay close attention to your thoughts, feelings, and how you react to different situations."

After a week, Pedro returned to the session with his completed emotional monitoring journal and showed it to the psychologist.

Emotional monitoring

	Mon day	Tues day	Wedne sday	Thurs day	Frid ay	Satur day	Sund ay
Morning							
Happy	😃	😃	😃	😃	😃	😃	😃
Neutral	😐	😐	😐	😐	😐	😐	😐
Sad	😞	😞	😞	😞	😞	😞	😞
Stressed/Anxious	😠	😠	😠	😠	😠	😠	😠
Afternoon							
Happy	😃	😃	😃	😃	😃	😃	😃
Neutral	😐	😐	😐	😐	😐	😐	😐
Sad	😞	😞	😞	😞	😞	😞	😞
Stressed/Anxious	😠	😠	😠	😠	😠	😠	😠
Evening							
Happy	😃	😃	😃	😃	😃	😃	😃
Neutral	😐	😐	😐	😐	😐	😐	😐

| Sad | ☹ | ☹ | ☹ | ☹ | ☹ | ☹ | ☹ |
| Stressed/Anxious | 😠 | 😠 | 😠 | 😠 | 😠 | 😠 | 😠 |

Situation:	Thoughts:
I noticed that I usually get more stressed and anxious in the morning when I remember I have to go to work. Throughout the day, I become more neutral, unless there's a problem at work, like my boss constantly demanding things, which happened on Wednesday, Thursday, and Friday. In the evening, I'm generally happier because I'm at home and can play games or watch series. "On Wednesday, my boss made me so irritated that I felt bad until the evening at home, constantly blaming myself for things I couldn't deliver at the moment. "I feel down on Sunday nights because I know I	Depends on the day. In the morning, I usually think, 'ugh, I wish I didn't have to work, I wish I could stay home peacefully, do something else I enjoy.' When my boss keeps nagging me, I think about quitting because it irritates me so much. On Friday mornings, I think, 'just one more day until I can rest,' and on weekends, I think, 'wonderful, finally I can relax, do my things, go out, etc.

have to go to work Monday morning.	

Psychologist:

- Perfect, now we have a better understanding of what's been bothering you. It seems mainly related to work, so we can think of ways for you to better handle this area. For example, considering possibilities to talk with your boss, trying to make him understand that you are very busy. But besides that, we also need to think about well-being practices.

1st Meditation and Mindfulness: Set aside a few minutes of your day to meditate or practice mindfulness. This can help reduce stress, increase concentration, and promote an overall sense of calm and balance.

Meditation involves focusing the mind on an object, thought, or specific activity to achieve mental clarity, relaxation, and full awareness of the present moment.

Mindfulness is the practice of being consciously aware and attentive to the present moment, accepting it without judgment.

2nd Physical Exercise: Engage in regular physical activities such as walking, running, yoga, swimming, or any other form of exercise you enjoy. Exercise not only improves physical health but can also elevate mood and reduce anxiety. Regular exercise strengthens muscles, improves cardiovascular health, and releases endorphins, neurotransmitters responsible for feelings of happiness. Besides physical benefits, regular exercise can enhance self-esteem, aid in stress management, and promote better sleep. Variety is key, so try different types of exercises to find what you enjoy most and stay motivated.

3rd Healthy Eating: Take care of your diet by prioritizing nutritious and balanced foods. A diet rich in fruits, vegetables, whole grains, and lean proteins provides essential nutrients for optimal body function and mental health. A balanced diet supplies vital vitamins for both body and mind. Emphasize whole foods such as fruits, vegetables, whole grains, lean proteins, and healthy fats, while limiting processed foods, added sugars, and unhealthy fats. Staying hydrated is also crucial for proper body and brain function.

4th Quality Time with Friends and Family: Set aside time to be with loved ones who support you.

Positive social relationships are essential for emotional well-being and can provide a sense of belonging and connection. Dedicate time to nurture meaningful relationships through deep conversations, shared activities, or simply being present for others. Spend more time with family and friends, whether it's through a simple message, a phone call, or being physically present by going for walks, traveling, or engaging in activities together.

5th Adequate Rest: Ensure you get enough sleep every night. Sleep plays a crucial role in both physical and mental health, aiding in recovery, information processing, cell regeneration, memory consolidation, and mood regulation. Try to establish a consistent sleep routine and create an environment conducive to a good night's rest. Establishing a consistent sleep routine, creating a sleep-friendly environment, and adopting relaxing bedtime practices such as meditation or reading, as well as practicing good sleep hygiene, can improve sleep quality.

6th Hobbies and Creative Activities: Dedicate time to activities that bring you joy and satisfaction, such as hobbies, art, music, reading, or any other form of creative expression you enjoy. These activities can serve as an outlet for everyday stress and provide moments of pleasure and relaxation.

Engaging in activities that bring you joy and satisfaction can reduce stress, boost self-esteem, and promote a sense of accomplishment. Hobbies and creative activities also stimulate the mind, encouraging creativity, personal expression, and ongoing learning.

Psychologist:

- These practices are very important to help regulate mood and reduce emotional fluctuations. If you need more guidance on nutrition, physical activities, consider consulting specific professionals such as nutritionists, personal trainers, among others, so you can receive tailored advice. After adopting these practices and continuing to monitor his emotions, Pedro began to better manage his emotions and achieve greater emotional stability and well-being. He had been engaging in beneficial activities for his body and mind, and his doctor also prescribed some vitamins to replenish those that were low.

Chapter VII

I think therefore it's real?

Did you know that throughout the day we have thousands of thoughts? Are all these thoughts we have real thoughts, or do we have mistaken thoughts about certain situations? Let me explain more about what I mean by this.

Often, we go through daily situations that generate some discomfort, stress, anxiety, sadness, among others, but not all these thoughts are necessarily real. And by saying this, I don't mean that you are delusional or anything like that, but often the interpretation we have of the situation can be distorted.

Two people can go to the same party; one may find the party excellent while the other may find it horrible. Why is that? Because each person has different experiences, different backgrounds, and they see and deal with situations differently based on their life history. That's why it's crucial to analyze how we are interpreting situations. Just because you think something doesn't necessarily mean it's true.

In the face of daily situations, we have automatic thoughts, which are thoughts that simply pop into our minds and we don't have control over. These thoughts can be termed dysfunctional thoughts, which are thoughts that you don't necessarily have evidence for being real, and they are mistaken, possibly even distorted thoughts. I'll explain more about this later.

Lucas began to feel much better after therapy sessions and emotional regulation practices. His anxiety reduced, and he managed to sleep better. However, some issues still bothered him—thoughts, worries:

- What if that thing happens?
- Is that person mad at me?
- What if I'm not good enough?

Something that happened very often was that during work hours, at least once a week, Lucas' boss called him for a meeting using the same phrases:

- "Let's talk in my office later."
- "I need to speak with you later."

No matter what he was doing, he would immediately start feeling nervous, anxious, and agitated. He would think things like:

- "Did I do something wrong?"
- "Is she going to scold me or fire me?"

Even if he had been through these situations before and nothing of the sort had happened. In other words, his mind started creating hypotheses and worries, scenarios, even though he had no evidence that these things would happen, which caused a lot of discomfort and anxiety.

When Lucas mentioned this to the psychologist, he began to explain how our minds work and why these types of thoughts occur.

Psychologist:

- Our minds have thousands of thoughts throughout the day, and when we encounter specific situations, these thoughts can often generate some discomfort. I'll explain how our "Cognitive Model" works, a term used in Cognitive Behavioral Therapy (CBT) to describe how perceptions of events influence our emotions and behaviors. First, there's a specific Situation, for example: The person you like is taking a long time to reply to your message. Next, there's the automatic thought: Why are they taking so long to respond? Maybe they don't like me, or perhaps I did something wrong. Are they upset or angry with me? Emotion: Sadness, anger. Behavior: Putting the phone aside, leaving, or isolating oneself, feeling upset. Emotions can also trigger physiological reactions, such as anxiety symptoms like palpitations, difficulty breathing, a feeling of distress, and tightness in the chest. After identifying the Situation, Thought, Emotion, and Behavior, we need to start working on these automatic thoughts because they can be dysfunctional. So, the psychologist asked Lucas:

- How much do you believe in this thought, from 0% to 100%?

Lucas:

- 90%.

Psychologist:

- So, you don't believe in this thought 100%, but even if you did, let's reflect a bit more on it. What was the intensity of the emotion you felt at the time?

Lucas:

- 90%, it was very strong. I felt really bad and didn't want to do anything else that day.

Psychologist:

- I understand. Now let's analyze these thoughts a bit more. Can you tell me if there are any evidences in favor or against these thoughts?

Lucas:

Well, evidences in favor... I can't think of any. I don't remember doing anything to make her upset with me or not want to talk to me. Evidences against, I can think that she might be busy, maybe she's working, and it's happened before where she didn't reply right away but later did and even apologized for the delay. And afterward, she talked to me normally, so she wasn't angry or sad with me.

Psychologist:

- Now, looking back at the situation, how do you feel about it and your thoughts?

Lucas:

- It seems like I overreacted, I think my emotions got the better of me.

Psychologist:

- Now, from 0% to 100%, how much do you believe in your thoughts that "She doesn't like you, or that you might have done something wrong, and that she is upset or angry with you?"

Lucas:

Now I believe 0%, because I realized I ended up exaggerating my thoughts and my reaction.

Analyzing the DTR or "Dysfunctional Thought Record" is a very important technique that helps you reframe your thoughts and how you perceive life and situations. That's why I'll leave the exercise so you can follow this step-by-step process.

Situation:	Thought:	Emotion:	Behavior:
How much do you believe in this from 0% to 100%?________________ _______		What is the intensity of this emotion from 0% to 100%?____________	

What are the evidences supporting this thought?

____
____
____
____

____

____

____

What are the evidences against this
thought?______________________________

____

____

____

____

____

____

How much do you believe in that previous thought now? _______________ ______	Do you feel a new emotion now?_______________ _______________
What would be a new thought?____________ ____________ _______________ ______ _______________ ______ _______________ ______	What new emotion do you feel now?_______________ ____________ _______________ ______ _______________ ______ _______________ ______

Cognitive Distortions

Cognitive distortions are common patterns of thought found in people that influence how we perceive situations. It's important to understand if your thoughts fall into any of these distortions so that we can find ways to deal with them. Here are some of the most common cognitive distortions:

Catastrophizing:

- Thinking that the worst possible outcome of a situation will occur, without considering the possibility of other outcomes. Believing that what will happen or has happened will be terrible and unbearable. Negative events that may occur are treated as intolerable catastrophes rather than being seen in perspective. Examples: "Losing my job will be the end of my career." "I won't be able to handle my wife leaving me." "If I lose control, it will be my downfall."

Polarization (Black-and-White Thinking):

- Viewing a situation only in two categories, mutually exclusive, the classic all-or-nothing mindset. Perceiving events or people in absolute terms. Examples: "Everything went wrong at the party." "I must always get the highest grade, or I'll be a failure." "It's either perfect or not worth it."

"Everyone rejects me." "It was a complete waste of time."

Selective Abstraction:

- Focusing on one aspect of a complex situation while ignoring other relevant aspects. Highlighting a negative (or even neutral) part of an entire situation while disregarding all positive aspects. Examples: "Look at all the people who don't like me." "My boss's evaluation was bad" (focusing only on one negative comment and neglecting all positive feedback).

Mind Reading:

Assuming, without evidence, that you know what others are thinking, disregarding other possible hypotheses. Examples: "She doesn't like my conversation." "He thinks I'm bothering him." "He didn't like my project."

Should Statements:

- Interpreting events in terms of how things should be instead of simply considering how things are. Making absolute statements in an attempt to motivate or modify behavior. Demands made on oneself, others, and the world to avoid the consequences of not meeting these demands. Examples: "I must have control over everything."

"I should be perfect in everything I do." "I shouldn't be bothered by my wife."

What Ifs:

- Focusing on what could have been but wasn't. Blaming oneself for past choices and questioning future decisions. Examples: "If I had taken the other job, I would be better off now." "What if the new job doesn't work out?" "If I hadn't traveled, this wouldn't have happened."

Identifying if you fit into any of these distortions helps in reframing these thoughts and prevents the feeling of "am I the only one who thinks this way?" You can realize that these are common thoughts among many people, enabling you to have tools to deal with these distortions.

Now you might be wondering, how do you deal with these distortions? There are several ways to work on changing this way of seeing situations.

1st: Use the "Dysfunctional Thought Record" (DTR), identify the distortion, and then point out the evidence for and against these thoughts.

2nd: Use the following Socratic Questioning to seek different ways of thinking about situations, which is a technique that will give you a new perspective and help you reframe your understanding of the situations.

Socratic Questioning:

- What evidence supports this idea?
- What evidence contradicts this idea?

    Alternative Interpretations:

- How would someone who does not feel or think like you react?
- What advice would you give to another person?
- Is there another thought that explains the same situation? Is there an alternative explanation?
- What evidence supports these alternatives?

    Realism:

- What is your goal in this situation?
- Does this thought help or hinder you in achieving your goal?

    Decatastrophizing:

- What is the worst that could happen if this thought is true? Can I overcome this?
- What is the best that could happen?
- What is the most realistic outcome?

After the psychologist provided this information to Lucas, he identified that Catastrophizing and the

"What If?" scenario were the most predominant. Therefore, the psychologist asked him to start working on Decatastrophizing and reflecting on the "What If?" thoughts.

Lucas:

- My initial thought was that I will score zero on the test and fail, thus having to retake the course.

- What is the worst that could happen if this thought is true? Can I overcome this? If this thought is true, it would be terrible because failing would delay my graduation, and my parents would argue with me a lot. But it wouldn't be the end of the world because I could try to pay for a retake and then study more.

- What is the best that could happen? I could score a perfect 10 and pass the course easily.

- What is the most realistic outcome? Well, I studied as much as possible, so I don't think I would score zero. Maybe I could get a 6, which is the minimum passing grade, especially since I didn't do so badly on other tests in this course.

- Now, regarding the "What If?" scenario, a situation that happened recently was me thinking, "What if when I graduate I don't like the field I chose and regret it, wanting to work in another area and feeling like I wasted time studying for this field?"

Psychologist:

- Now, thinking about Socratic questioning, "What advice would you give to someone else in the same situation as yours?"

Lucas:

- I would say, calm down, you're suffering in advance, there's still some time until you graduate, and even if you don't like the field you're in, you can pursue another degree later on, or explore other job possibilities. Try to live one day at a time and leave that worry to future Lucas.

These are just a few examples of possibilities we have to deal with everyday situations, our thoughts, and concerns. Try to adapt these tools and techniques to your reality.

Now, something I often hear is:

- Rationally, I understand these points, but when I'm in the situation, I feel really bad, uncomfortable with these thoughts. This is precisely because often those thoughts are already deeply ingrained, they're internalized, and sometimes even become beliefs. One way to deal with these thoughts and feelings is through reinforcement. Humans operate a lot on reinforcement, for example: If someone tells you you're stupid, incapable, for a long time, you end up believing it's true, internalizing it, and it becomes a belief, you think it's true because you've heard it so many times. At this point, it's important to talk about something very powerful in our lives, which are some core beliefs that we can develop over the course of life.

Helplessness Belief. The person sees themselves and believes to be extremely vulnerable, fragile, needy, maladjusted, or even inadequate. For example, some automatic thoughts stemming from this belief are: "I am alone; I can't do this"; "I can't do this alone"; "I can't change"; "I don't know/can't defend myself"; "I don't know how to do things for myself"; "I'll never learn to do this."

Unloved Belief. The person feels unworthy of love, undesirable, with defects that are impossible to improve, imperfect, impossible to be accepted, unattractive, rejected. Some recurring thoughts from this belief include: "Who would want to love someone like me"; "No one will ever like me"; "I'm not good enough to be loved and desired"; "I will always be rejected"; "I'll never find anyone"; "No one will want to be with me"; "I'll be alone forever"; "No one notices me."

Worthlessness Belief. The person cannot see/feel value in themselves or in anything they do. Automatic thoughts include: "I'm worthless"; "I'm a failure"; "I don't deserve to succeed"; "I have nothing good to offer"; "I'm worthless"; "I'm useless"; "I never do anything right"; "I'm not very smart"; "I won't succeed"; "I don't deserve to win/be successful/be happy."

Now, how is it possible to modify these beliefs through reinforcement? There's a very important technique called **Coping Card**, and to use it you will do the following:

1st Identify the belief or thought that is bothering you in a situation, for example, let's take "I am dumb."

2nd You need to think about what supports or contradicts this thought.
Supporting evidence: My parents often told me in my childhood that I was dumb and wouldn't succeed in life.
Contradictory evidence: Despite having a bit more difficulty in school, I passed all my subjects, never had to retake any exams, and now in college I manage to score well on tests; my classmates even ask me for help studying.

Now let's create the Coping Card as follows, let's put a title and then what we need to reinforce for our mind, for example:

Coping Card for "I am dumb."

I know I'm not dumb because I get good grades in college, people ask me for help on how to study and do well on tests; I usually score at least 8 on exams. Moreover, when I was a child I never had to retake exams or repeat a year, so these beliefs of being dumb are not true, they were implanted by my parents who wanted to put me down and demanded too much from me.

After writing this Coping Card, what you need to do is read it whenever this type of thought comes to your mind, because this way you will internalize this new way of thinking and it will become part of your new beliefs. Depending on how deeply rooted these beliefs are, it may take you longer to change them, but always remember reinforcement, that is, the more you reinforce that to your mind, the easier it will be for you to internalize these new ways of thinking.

Chapter VII

Problem Solving

Certainly one of the words we hear most in our daily lives, whether at work or at home, is "problems" (no wonder it's the title of this book). It doesn't matter the quantity of problems; it could be just one, or several — health problems, financial problems — but it's something that is very present in people's lives.

These problems generate a lot of disruptions, anxiety, stress, depression, among other things. Now, something very important in our lives is how to deal with them. You can either let them take over your life, feeling defeated, accepting that these problems are knocking you down, or you can try to do something to solve these problems.

Do you have control about them?
Pedro (Fictitious name), 50 years old, has always suffered a lot trying to have control over situations and problems. This caused a lot of anxiety and anguish because when something got "out of control," he felt frustrated because things didn't go as expected. In various situations, whether professional or personal, he wanted to have control over everything.

Before specifically addressing the problems, it's important to analyze: Is this problem something I can modify, influence, or not? Is it something beyond my reach? If it's beyond your control to solve that problem, we need to work towards acceptance — not passive acceptance, but an understanding that everything within your reach has been done.

When Pedro arrived at the psychologist's office, he reported:

Pedro:

- My 73-year-old mother is driving me crazy. She has various health problems, feels pain, has anxiety, depression. Many years ago, she used to take care of herself, go to doctors, do physical activities, go to psychologists and psychiatrists. After a while, she didn't want anything to do with that anymore. Nowadays, she eats poorly, smokes, stays at home all day, and this makes me very sad. I've tried taking her to doctors, but she doesn't want to go. I've tried asking for help from my siblings; I have a brother and a sister who are also concerned about her situation.

Psychologist:

- I understand it's a very worrying situation, especially because it depends not only on you but mainly on your mother herself. It's like hitting your head against a wall; you're trying to help her, but she's not interested. How do you feel about this?

Pedro:

- I feel like a failure. I feel like I've done everything, but it's not enough. I want to find a way to be able to help her, I want to do something more.

Psychologist:

- Yes, especially when it involves close people, family, and especially your mother, it generates a very strong concern and frustration. It can even create a sense of guilt, as if you're not doing enough.

Pedro:

- Exactly!

Psychologist:

- But a very important point to keep in mind is that situations are not always within our control. You've tried and are still trying your best. You've talked to her, you've asked for help from your siblings, but she doesn't want to accept this help. As much as she's not well, she's "comfortable" with this situation. I'm not saying you should give up and stop trying to do anything to help her, but carrying this feeling of guilt is harmful to you because it's not like you haven't done anything.

Pedro:

- Wow, that's true. I hadn't thought about that. I've tried practically everything to resolve this situation, to help her, but she remains the same, and it's her choice, as you said. I'm trying everything, putting in effort. I've spent sleepless nights thinking about how to help her, how to solve this problem, but I still haven't found a solution.

Psychologist:

- Even though you've tried many solutions, there might be something you haven't thought of yet. Let's try a problem-solving strategy. I'll give you an exercise, and I'd like you to do it, either alone or even with your siblings, to try to find a solution to this situation.

Pedro:

- Perfect, I'm open to all possibilities to try to solve this problem!

Problem Solving

What is the problem or concern?

What are the consequences of not being able to solve your problem? And the benefits of being able to solve it?

Think about possible solutions to this problem, regardless of whether they seem good or bad.	Advantages of this solution:	Disadvantages of this solution:

This is a technique that may seem simple, but it is very effective in solving various types of problems because, in addition to stopping and reflecting on the problem, there is a written part that greatly helps in visualizing the problem and possible solutions in a more concrete way.

After doing this exercise, Pedro came back the following week feeling more optimistic because he had managed to think of some solutions and even put some into practice.

What is the problem or concern?
A: The physical and mental health of my mother.

What are the consequences of not being able to solve your problem? And the benefits of achieving it?
A: If not solved, she will worsen over time and the worst could happen. If solved, she will become healthier and happier, which will be very good for all of us.

Think about possible solutions to this problem, no	Advantages of this solution	Disadvantages of this solution

matter if they seem good or bad.		
Try to "tie her up" and forcibly drag her to the doctors.	At least she would undergo the necessary exams and see the doctors she needs.	It would create a lot of confusion. She would become very nervous and it could lead to a big fight with all of us.
Try talking to her once more, explaining why it's important for her to seek treatment, expressing how much we love her, and how much we suffer seeing her like this.	Perhaps she will agree to see a doctor and take care of herself. This approach could directly benefit her health and strengthen our bonds.	None

Pedro:

- This exercise helped a lot. I thought about what I could do to help her, talked to my siblings, and they thought it was great. Last Saturday, we went to her house and tried to talk to her calmly. We brought photos from when she was younger, showed how joyful she used to be, how much fun we had together, and emphasized the importance of taking care of her health. We even cried with emotion. In the end, she agreed to seek help, see a psychologist and doctors. I've already started scheduling appointments, and I'll take her in the coming weeks. We are very happy, now it's just a matter of continuing on this path. Thank you very much, we were feeling hopeless about how to begin resolving this situation.

It's always important to evaluate whether the problem we want to solve is feasible or not. Always ask yourself, can I realistically solve this problem? Does it depend solely on my effort or also on others? There are situations where the problem depends on external factors that we cannot control. For example, if you're dealing with a work situation that requires collaboration from other people or departments, do these individuals want to cooperate?

Unfortunately, there are cases where people in other departments simply aren't interested or find it more convenient to continue as things are. This also applies to personal situations. In Pedro's case, he and his siblings were able to talk to their mother and she understood the importance of taking care of herself. However, there are cases where the person lacks this interest and prefers to continue as they are, no matter how much you try to explain why the current situation is harmful to them.

The Importance of an Action Plan

Once we've identified a potential solution to a particular problem, we need to consider how to put it into practice. What are the next steps to actually resolve that problem?

Pedro was also facing an issue in his accounting firm where he wasn't able to acquire new clients. People would inquire about pricing and services but often wouldn't follow through. He used problem-solving tools to identify potential solutions and began strategizing on how to improve these aspects. He created the following action plan:

1. Research marketing and entrepreneurship courses.
2. Research competitors.
3. Analyze if there are any issues with his website or landing page.

4. Assess if his pricing is competitive.
5. Research consulting services that could help his company.
6. Implement what he learns from courses and consulting.

He started implementing this action plan and after a few months, he noticed significant improvements. He identified issues with his website, customer service, and how he explained the importance of his services to potential clients, which led to increased revenue.

In summary, when faced with a problem, simply enduring it won't suffice, even if it causes significant discomfort. We need to identify if it's something that can be resolved and, if so, consider what actions we can take to address it promptly, preventing it from lingering for too long.

Chapter IX

Do you know how to communicate, or just speak?

There is a difference between knowing how to communicate and merely speaking. When you only speak, you might end up saying things you didn't mean, hurting others or even yourself. There's a kind of communication intelligence that helps us not only understand what to say but also how to say it.

Have you ever heard or experienced this? "That's not what I meant" or "I said X and the person understood Y." Sometimes, you may know what you want to say but not how the other person will interpret it. While this often reflects more on the other person than on yourself, it's important to communicate as clearly as possible to avoid misunderstandings.

One of the pillars of any relationship is communication, whether it's a romantic relationship like dating or marriage, or relationships with family, friends, or business partners. All relationships are based on communication: "No communication, no relationship."

Jonas (fictional name) and Fabiana (fictional name) have been married for 5 years but are struggling to coexist. They don't know whether to continue or file for divorce.

They decided to seek a psychologist for couples therapy.

Fabiana:

- Jonas's problem is that when something bothers him, he stays quiet. I ask him, "Is something wrong? Did I do something that upset you?" And he says no, everything is fine, but he looks upset, like he ate something he didn't like.

Jonas:

- Fabiana gets nervous and takes it out on me whenever anything happens. If she has a problem at work, she comes home very stressed and picks fights over anything. A few times I tried to talk about something bothering me, she ended up arguing with me, calling me names, so I decided to stay quiet.

Fabiana:

- But that really irritates me. Okay, I understand I may overreact sometimes and take it out on you, but if you don't tell me what's bothering you, I won't know!

Psychologist:

- Alright, I see that your communication is indeed quite flawed, or almost nonexistent. This is very detrimental to any kind of relationship, but especially to a marriage. You need to be able to express what you're feeling without fear of judgment, so that you can understand each other.

We need to work on your communication as well as other issues like stress. First, I want you to start practicing emotional regulation techniques such as breathing, grounding, and mindfulness (Chapter V). Then, we need to work on your communication. Psychology studies various forms of behavior and communication, but there are four that are very present in daily life. I will explain them to you and then I want to know if you identify with one or more of them.

Passive Communication:

Passive communication occurs when a person has difficulty asserting themselves, expressing what they feel and think, and often sets aside their own rights. This type of communication can lead to self-harm out of fear of displeasing others or causing conflicts. For example: If someone is invited to go to a park but actually doesn't want to go and can't say NO, they end up in an uncomfortable situation they didn't want to be in, which can leave them feeling sad, anxious, stressed, and frustrated because they accepted something they didn't want.

Aggressive Communication:

Aggressive communication involves speaking in a harsh, rude manner that hurts others, leaving them sad and causing more stress and arguments. A person may learn this communication style through their upbringing or daily stress, making it important to understand its origins.

Passive-Aggressive Communication:

In this type of communication, a person may appear calm and passive but communicates in a way that can be subtly harsh, using sarcasm or irony that may go unnoticed. This behavior can also create discomfort and drive people away.

Assertive Communication:

Assertive communication is considered ideal because it allows individuals to express their feelings and rights while respecting others' feelings. It's a balanced communication style that doesn't harm any party involved, making it crucial to develop.

It's important to note that no one uses one type of communication exclusively at all times. Individuals may switch between assertive, passive, and aggressive communication styles depending on the situation. Recognizing which communication style you use is the first step in developing more effective communication skills.

I'll use a practical example so you can better understand each communication style.

Let's imagine you're presenting a work meeting, but someone disagrees with you and even shows rudeness towards you. How would you react to this situation?

First, **passive communication:** "Oh, I see. Maybe what I said didn't make much sense. I should have thought of another issue to discuss, or said it differently."

Aggressive communication: "Listen, I don't care what you think or what you're saying. I'm tired of you constantly interrupting my presentations and saying that what I say doesn't make sense."

Passive-aggressive communication: "Yeah, sure, I understand. Well, at least I did my part, unlike some people."

Assertive communication: "Thank you for sharing your opinion. I see things differently because I've researched this topic and reached these conclusions after careful analysis. However, your perspective is valuable too."

Psychologist:

- Can you identify which types of communication you tend to use?

Jonas:

- I lean towards passive communication most of the time. I often keep things to myself and struggle to say no.

Fabiana:

- I'm more on the aggressive and passive-aggressive side, but at work, I can be assertive because I'm a manager and deal with many people daily.

Psychologist:

- Now that you've identified the main types of communication you use, we need to work on how you can learn to communicate differently.

So, I'll leave you with an exercise that you can use to start working on your communication style:

What was the situation you went through?			
How did you react to this situation? Were you:			
Passive	Agressive	Passive Agressive	Assertive

Now, write how you could have reacted to the situation in an assertive manner.			

By doing this exercise, the couple began to understand where they were going wrong in their communication and started reflecting on various different situations, considering how they could act differently.

In addition to these practical exercises, it's important to keep in mind some key points that make a difference. For instance, when we think about passive behavior, we need to remember our rights and why it's important to assert ourselves and say no. Below, I will provide a list of rights for you to begin reflecting on and remembering the rights we need to keep in mind in our daily lives to live a healthier life.

List of Basic Human Rights:

- The right to maintain your dignity and respect—even if it displeases someone, as long as it does not violate the rights of others.

- The right to be treated with consideration and dignity.
- The right to refuse requests without feeling guilty or selfish.
- The right to experience and express your own feelings.
- The right to pause and reflect before taking action.
- The right to change your mind.
- The right to ask for what you want (knowing that others have the right to refuse).
- The right to do less than you are capable of.
- The right to be independent.
- The right to decide what to do with your body, time, and property.
- The right to request information.
- The right to make mistakes—and take responsibility for them.
- The right to feel good about yourself.
- The right to have your own needs and have them be as important as others'.
- The right to ask (not demand) that others meet your needs.
- The right to decide whether to meet the needs of others.
- The right to act in your own interests—as long as it does not violate the rights of others.
- The right to have opinions and express them.

- The right to decide whether to meet others' expectations.
- The right to discuss problems with the person involved and clarify them when rights are not clear.
- The right to receive what was paid for.
- The right to choose not to behave in the most appropriate way.
- The right to have rights and defend them.
- The right to be heard and taken seriously.
- The right to be alone when you want to be.
- The right to do anything as long as it does not violate the rights of others.

Now you can read this list of rights every day, as constant reinforcement is very important to internalize the concepts and to get used to putting them into practice.

How to deal with aggressive communication and behavior? You can develop a habit of practicing relaxation and emotional regulation techniques so that you get used to not reacting in a way you'll later regret. When you notice you're becoming stressed and might react aggressively or passively aggressively, try to breathe, leave the environment, get some water, or go to the bathroom, and reflect. Ask yourself, would what I was about to say hurt or harm the other person? Then reconsider how you would communicate and return to the situation with a calmer mind.

I know it's difficult to put this kind of automatic response into practice, especially if you're used to communicating in ways that aren't assertive, but the more you practice, the easier it will become. You can also try writing reminders on your phone or on post-its like "Reminder for assertive communication."

After some time analyzing situations, the couple realized their communication was very flawed and they needed to continue working to improve how they interacted with each other and with others.

Fabiana:

- Our relationship is much better now. I can stop before reacting to situations, reflect on the situation and how I'll react to it. This has helped me not only in my relationship with Jonas but also at work, and with family and friends. Now I'm even more sociable.

Jonas:

- Yes, she has improved a lot, and now I feel more comfortable expressing what's bothering me without fear of reproach. I've learned that if I don't speak up, I'm the one who suffers the most, so I've been trying to be as assertive as possible.

Psychologist:

- Perfect, little by little you'll get used to assertive communication and turn it into a habit. The important thing is always to bring it into awareness and reinforce the benefits of assertive communication.

Chapter X

Difficulty with weight loss and addictions

Do you think people struggling to lose weight and those with some type of addiction have something in common? I'll show you that they have very important common points, and in most cases, these are emotional issues.

Fernanda (fictional name), 29 years old, was weighing 100kg at 1.70m tall, classified as obese. According to her nutritionist, she should weigh around 70kg, which means 30kg less. She has undergone various treatments, seen nutritionists, specialists in nutritional medicine, and tried working out with a personal trainer, but all in vain. She could lose weight temporarily, but would gain it back later, sometimes even more. Because no matter what she did or took, she wasn't addressing the root cause—she gained weight because she used food as a coping mechanism, eating without hunger. But why did she do this? It was then, with guidance, that she decided to seek help from a psychologist.

Fernanda:

- I don't know what else to do anymore. I suffer from yo-yo dieting; I lose weight, gain it back several times. I can't maintain a stable weight. I turn to food, I "raid the fridge" at night, sometimes I eat much more than I need and then feel terrible about it. Sometimes I even cry and wonder, why can't I control my eating? I have a food compulsion.

Psychologist:

- I understand. Has this been happening for a while, or has it always been like this?

Fernanda:

- Actually, no. When I was younger, I was very thin. But after a breakup from a 6-year relationship, I started using food as a coping mechanism and felt very bad, and that's when the yo-yo dieting started.

Psychologist:

- How would you describe your emotional state nowadays? Are you anxious, stressed?

Fernanda:

- I'm extremely anxious, stressed, I easily argue with people, can't sit still, always thinking about the future and worrying about what might happen. If I have an important work meeting or a presentation at college, I can't even sleep properly.

Psychologist:

- I see. When we think about compulsions, not just eating but also other addictions like gaming, drugs, or alcohol, we often consider them as an escape valve. It's something related to our emotional state not being well, and we end up using food or something else to cope. When you eat a lot without being hungry, it's like you're trying to fill a void.

And we often say that our stomach is like a second brain. When we eat, especially foods we really enjoy, we feel a pleasant sensation, we become more relaxed because of the release of "pleasure hormones" like serotonin, among others. The problem is, this pleasant feeling doesn't last long, which is why you feel the need to eat over and over again, even when not hungry. So, before trying to reduce your food compulsion, we need to address the root cause, which is your emotions, so that you can feel calmer, more relaxed, and not rely on food as an escape valve.

Fernanda:

- That's exactly how I feel. I eat very quickly, often while watching a series, I eat without being hungry, especially when I eat sweets that I love. It makes me feel calmer, but then the effect wears off and I become anxious and stressed again, which makes me want to eat more.

Psychologist:

- First of all, I want to teach you some emotional regulation techniques. Among them are 5x5x5 breathing, Muscle Contraction, and Mindfulness (Chapter V), specifically Mindfulness during meal times. We need to lower these levels of anxiety and stress, and you need to feel more relaxed, calmer.

When we think about food compulsion, one of the main points is working on the feeling of satiety because if you eat too quickly, your brain doesn't have time to interpret the feeling of that food. So, when you're eating out of hunger and you eat quickly, you'll still feel hungry. That's why it's important to eat slowly, savor your food.

Additionally, when you feel like eating, try to identify if you really need to eat because you're hungry, or if it's just a desire to eat to feel relieved. If it's not real hunger, try doing the breathing exercises, drink water or tea; this will also help.

Fernanda:

- Okay, I'll try to put these practices into action, and I'll report back on what I managed to do in the next session.

The following week, Fernanda returned to the session with some positive changes.

Fernanda:

- I've been putting into practice the techniques you gave me, but if I said it was easy, I'd be lying. The part about staying quiet and focusing on my breathing, eating slowly, is really hard. When I try to pay attention to the food, my mind wanders, and I have to keep bringing my focus back to the moment of eating. But at least I managed to eat more slowly and leave my phone aside. I used muscle contraction a lot because it was a stressful week at work, and I also used the breathing exercises and felt calmer. I did it before bed, and it helped, but I still wake up many times during the night with a restless mind.

Psychologist:

- Excellent, change happens gradually, especially because you're not used to doing activities calmly, relaxing. For you, being anxious and stressed is natural, so now you need to change your habits, and that takes time. But the fact that you've started putting things into practice is very important. Regarding sleep, you can use the Sleep Hygiene technique (Chapter V), which will also help you have better sleep quality and feel more relaxed.

Throughout the sessions, the psychologist and Fernanda worked on various aspects like thoughts, assertive communication, emotional regulation, micro-steps, and micro-goals. She started feeling calmer and learned to handle situations that used to stress her out better.

The psychologist also addressed the initial issue that triggered her yo-yo effect, which was the end of her 6-year relationship. She mentioned feeling nothing towards him anymore, not even anger; he was just a distant memory. However, she discovered it had been an abusive relationship, and despite him not having any direct influence on her anymore, she was left with some emotional scars, low self-esteem, and a sense of devaluation. This is very common in people struggling with weight loss or compulsive behaviors, especially because society often devalues those who carry a few extra pounds.

Therefore, it was also crucial to work on improving her self-esteem during the sessions. The psychologist advised Fernanda to make a list of her physical and personality qualities and start reading it daily to reinforce these aspects.

Physical qualities	Personality qualities
Beautiful smile	Hardworking
Eyes	Sincere
Beautiful hair	I like to help others
Beautiful hands	I get good grades

She began to repeat this list every day, and it started to bring a very positive feeling to her because she knew these qualities were real and made her feel special.

And now, what are your qualities? Make a list too.

After working on these aspects for a few months, she started feeling more relieved, her self-esteem improved, she became more upbeat, followed the diet prescribed by the nutritionist, engaged in physical activity, and gradually managed to lose weight, reaching 70kg. Of course, this process wasn't magical, happening overnight, but once she became aware that her food compulsion was a coping mechanism with emotional roots and through collaborative work with the psychologist, it became possible to address the issues that had been bothering her. Eventually, she no longer needed to turn to food as an escape to feel satisfied. She was able to confront her problems and handle day-to-day situations and past traumas in a more functional way.

Now you may be wondering, okay, but you mentioned that addictions like drinking, gambling, drugs, etc., are related to the difficulty in losing weight and food compulsion. Please explain more about this.

As mentioned earlier, most of the time, compulsions or addictions serve as a coping mechanism, meaning they are related to emotional issues such as anxiety, stress, depression, or something the person is struggling to handle.

Therefore, it's extremely important to understand which emotion is causing these behaviors, what types of thoughts are involved, and what is bothering the person so that we can delve deeper and work to reduce their reliance on this coping mechanism.

Another important point to consider is the use of micro-steps and micro-goals. If you want to quit smoking, stop drinking, for example, trying to quit all at once can often be very difficult and even harmful.

Take André (fictional name), 37 years old, who has been smoking since he was 20. He has tried to quit several times and always attempted to quit smoking abruptly. He would think, "Tomorrow, I'm going to quit smoking for good," then he would stash away his cigarettes or even throw them out. Sometimes he managed to stay smoke-free for a few days or weeks, but when he smelled smoke, especially from people nearby smoking, he couldn't resist and would relapse.

Additionally, since he didn't address issues like anxiety and stress, he would become very nervous, anxious, and irritable, even arguing with people around him. There were times when he would swap one addiction for another, meaning he would quit smoking but start eating compulsively or even drinking frequently.

So, how do you manage to quit for good? First, we need to understand that becoming aware of the harm that addiction is causing you, regardless of what it is—alcohol, food, drugs—is crucial. The psychologist who was working with André advised him to make a list of the pros and cons of continuing with that addiction. This might seem strange because what could the pros possibly be?

But they do exist, so André made the list:

Pros	Cons
I feel calmer, and I forget about my problems.	It is very bad for my health.
It's easier for me to socialize.	I have difficulty doing physical activities and even walking; I get very tired.
I can take breaks at work to smoke.	Family and friends who don't smoke feel uncomfortable with the smell and even distance

	themselves.
	I am causing the people close to me to smoke indirectly.

Making a pros and cons list is an excellent technique because it allows you to reflect on the situation and the benefits and drawbacks of a certain behavior. Bringing this into your awareness is the first step toward changing these harmful habits.

You can also take this list of pros and cons and post it on your refrigerator, on your wardrobe door, or in your bedroom. If necessary, make several copies of this list and place them in different locations. This way, you will have a visual reminder and reinforce why you need to stop this addiction or compulsion.

Think in terms of small steps. If you smoke 10 cigarettes a day, drink 5 bottles of alcohol a day, or eat compulsively 6 times a day, start reducing gradually. For example, start smoking 9 times a day, practice the 5x5x5 breathing technique when you feel the urge to smoke, start practicing meditation, physical activities, or other activities that promote well-being. Work on what is bothering you and find ways to better handle daily situations and stresses.

Changing habits is also crucial when you want to quit addictions. For example, if you usually go to and from work on Street X, and there is a bar where you always stop after work to drink or smoke, your mind is conditioned to always stop there and feed the addiction. So, start changing your route to and from work. Take a different street, preferably one that is far away and doesn't have any bars.

If you usually go out with work friends to a place where you drink coffee and then eat sweets, talk to them and suggest going somewhere different, preferably a place where sweets are not easily accessible.

Moreover, if you don't buy food that is not part of your diet, cigarettes, or alcohol, it becomes easier to resist. When you're at home and feel the urge to consume something that feeds your addiction, you will have to make an extra effort to go out and buy it, increasing the chances that you'll stay home instead.

Evaluate the people around you. If you have people who don't support you, who drink, smoke, eat excessively, and think your efforts to stop are silly, talk to them assertively and explain why you need to do this. In some cases, when people don't understand the importance of these changes, we may even need to distance ourselves from certain individuals. I know this might seem drastic, but we need to prioritize ourselves and take care of our physical and mental health.

Take note of the small achievements. Often, we only value big accomplishments and overlook the small victories. Keep a list or even a diary and write things down, for example:

"Today, on xx/xx/xxxx, when I had the urge to eat a sweet, I managed to breathe, change my focus, and realized that I wasn't hungry, just wanted to eat. I resisted and didn't buy the sweet. I felt I had better control and stayed focused on my goal to lose weight. I was very happy with this small victory because now I know it's possible. I need to learn to manage my emotions and compulsions."

Similarly, if you slip up, be careful with self-criticism. It's very present in our daily lives and can make something simple seem like the end of the world. For example, let's say you've been following your diet correctly for 7 days and one day, you stray from it because you attended a birthday party with friends where there were many delicious things.

You might start to feel guilty, criticize yourself, and feel like you ruined your diet, thinking it's not worth it. Understand that slipping from your diet, smoking one more cigarette, or consuming more alcohol than you should doesn't mean all your progress is lost, or that you are a failure. It's normal to have ups and downs. That day might have been one where you felt more stressed, anxious, or overwhelmed, or you might have just given in to the pleasant feeling that old habit brought you. When a "slip" happens, try not to criticize yourself. Think:

"Well, I know I shouldn't have done that, but it's natural. I haven't completely changed my habit yet because it's a process, something that takes time. I understand that slipping from my plan doesn't mean I'm a failure, but that I'm human, with emotions and feelings. Tomorrow, I'll continue strong and firm in my purpose."

Then, read your list of pros and cons again to reinforce why you should continue on that path.

Chapter XI

How to Cope with GRIEF

Grief is generally associated with the death of someone close, whether a family member, friend, acquaintance, or even a pet. However, it is also a process that occurs with the end of various life cycles, such as the end of a relationship, leaving a job, or moving to a new home or city. Essentially, any significant ending, especially when one is unprepared, can generate grief.

The 5 Stages of Grief

When we talk about grief, there are five stages that people typically go through. The intensity and duration of each stage vary from person to person. Some may go through grief quickly, especially if they can express what they are feeling, while others may take longer, lasting days, weeks, months, or in some cases, even years.

The First Stage: Denial

When confronted with a loss, it is common for our first response to be denial. Instinctively, we resist the truth, convincing ourselves that the event has not occurred, as if it were just a terrible dream or something completely impossible. This reaction is a natural emotional defense, an attempt to shield ourselves from the pain that acceptance would bring. Therefore, we prefer to reject the painful reality, refusing to accept it.

The Second Stage: Anger

As a person begins to accept the reality of the loss, leaving the denial stage behind, a series of distinct emotions usually invade their inner self. These feelings can include guilt, fear, anguish, and anger. A sense of revolt against the situation arises, even after understanding the fact. The person may blame themselves for actions that could have been taken to change the course of events, leading to intense anguish. These feelings are extremely harmful and can negatively affect both the person experiencing grief and those around them.

The Third Stage: Bargaining

In the third stage of the grief process, a desperate attempt to recover what was lost emerges. At this stage, the person starts to think of ways to reverse the situation that led to the grief. In cases of death, they might want to bargain with God or spirituality, depending on their beliefs. In cases of relationship breakups, job loss, or other types of grief, the person may start making plans to try to recover what was lost, even seeking help from others who might intervene in some way. For example, in relationships, the person might make promises to change their behavior or improve.

The Fourth Stage: Depression

We can think of depression in this context as the moment when the person loses the strength to fight. They no longer want to bargain or feel anger, and they succumb to deep sadness. This sadness can last for weeks, months, or even years. It is a time when the pain and sense of loss resurface constantly through memories, thoughts, and places connected to the one who is gone. The void left by the absence is confronted, and profound loneliness and sadness become frequent companions. During grief-related depression, it is common to distance oneself from loved ones and activities that once brought pleasure. Changes in sleep and appetite, either increasing or decreasing, can occur. It is a time when the emptiness of the loss overflows in tears, whether internal or external.

The Fifth Stage: Acceptance

In this final stage of the grieving process, the individual comes to accept that what they once had is gone and will not return. While they may still feel sadness, it no longer paralyzes them. They understand that remaining in a prolonged state of grief is unproductive, and they recognize the need to move forward with their life. At this point, they begin to live again, with the memories of what was lost becoming less negative and impactful, turning instead into cherished memories of past

experiences, whether related to a person, a home,
or a job.

How Long is Grief Healthy?

This is an important question because, while it is
necessary to experience grief, it should not last
excessively long as it can lead to significant life
disruptions. There is no fixed or "right" duration for
grief, as it is a highly individual and variable
process. The time it takes for someone to move
through grief can depend on a variety of factors,
including the nature of the loss, available emotional
support, past experiences with loss, and even
cultural differences.

For some, the grieving process may be shorter,
lasting weeks or months, while for others it can last
years. However, when the person or those around
them notice that the grief is not subsiding and is
causing significant harm—for instance, if the
individual remains isolated, unable to live their life,
work, or engage in activities they once enjoyed,
and is stuck in the past—this indicates a problem.
In such cases, seeking professional help to manage
the grief process is essential.

At the same time, trying to rush or deny the
grieving process can be harmful. It is extremely
important to allow oneself to feel and express the
emotions associated with loss. Often, people want
to appear strong and courageous, avoiding the

grieving process, which leads to repressed emotions. This can cause issues such as anxiety, panic, unexplained crying, and even physical problems as the body reacts to these unexpressed feelings.

Amanda's Story (Fictional Name)

Amanda, a 45-year-old woman, lost her 72-year-old father to a heart attack. They lived in different states—he in Maranhão and she in São Paulo. They always had a great relationship, but after she got married, moved out, and had her children, her busy life prevented her from visiting her parents frequently. It had been six months since she last saw her father when she visited him for his birthday. She hadn't been able to spend time with him and her mother since then.

When she received news of his death, a flood of thoughts overwhelmed her. She questioned why she hadn't spent more time with him, lamented that he was still relatively young, and wondered if she could have helped in some way if she had visited more often, especially when he was ill. These thoughts filled her with guilt and disbelief, severely impacting her well-being. She began to suffer from anxiety attacks, insomnia, and difficulty concentrating at work. She oscillated between the first four stages of grief for months, unable to reach acceptance. This ongoing struggle led to various negative consequences, leaving her family unsure of how to help. Her husband and children felt exhausted, as her grief consumed her and disrupted their lives, until they finally decided to seek help from a psychologist.

Amanda agreed to seek therapy because she felt overwhelmed by the situation and wanted to improve, even though she had no idea how that could happen. In her therapy session, she shared her story with the psychologist, who immediately recognized she was suffering from prolonged grief. This type of grief extends over a long period, impacting various aspects of a person's life and hindering their ability to move forward.

Psychologist:

- I understand that you were very close to your father and had a strong friendship, making his loss incredibly difficult.

Amanda:

- I still can't believe he's gone. I won't be able to talk to him, see him at family gatherings, or even call him anymore. Sometimes it feels like he's still there, at their house, still alive.

Psychologist:

- Have you visited your mother since his passing?

Amanda:

- I haven't had the courage, and I also lack the energy to travel there.

Psychologist:

- This is a very important point for us to work on for the acceptance phase, which is the final stage of the grieving process.

Amanda:

- But I feel like if I go there and don't find him, it will be worse. I'll have the "certainty" that he's really gone.

Psychologist:

- I understand. However, by avoiding going there, you are in a cycle of avoidance. It's as if your mind is living in an illusion. This is a natural defense mechanism, a way for your mind to protect you from a situation that might make you uncomfortable.

Amanda:

- So, if I go there and face the situation, will I feel better?

Psychologist:

- It will be a crucial part of the acceptance process. But before you go, I want you to follow some steps and practice emotional regulation techniques. Then, focus on the good memories you had with him, the happy moments. Think about and write down all that he experienced. You mentioned you felt he left too soon, but how was his life?

Amanda:

- Well, he had three children, traveled a lot around Brazil and the world, had many friends, and did a lot of things. He enjoyed life a lot.

Psychologist:

- Does thinking about these things help you feel more at ease?

Amanda:

- Yes, a little. At least I don't feel like he didn't live his life. I know he did what he wanted to do. My mother says he fulfilled his mission. She's very religious, and that helped her cope with her grief.

Psychologist:

- And what do you believe?

Amanda:

- I believe he's in a better place and that while he was here, he did many good things and helped many people. He was a wonderful person.

Psychologist:

- That's very important too. You can write this down as well because writing it will reinforce these positive points.

Psychologist:

- You also mentioned feeling guilty, right?

Amanda:

- Yes, I feel guilty because I wanted to spend more time with him and be there when he was in the hospital, but because of work and the busyness of everyday life, I couldn't. The plane ticket was also very expensive.

Psychologist:

- I understand. These are situations beyond your control. From what you've told me, he had a heart attack one day, was hospitalized, and passed away the next day. You couldn't have prepared to go see him because, as you mentioned, the plane ticket was also an obstacle.

Another important point is that you couldn't have predicted his death. Despite the heart attack, your mother and brother said he didn't seem that bad, so it was unexpected. Has anyone in your family blamed you for not being there?

Amanda:

- No, everyone understood. The guilt and self-blame are entirely mine. But now that I think about it, I really couldn't have known he was going to die.

Psychologist:

- Exactly, just as you couldn't predict he would have a heart attack. When you visited him six months ago, he was fine, right?

Amanda:

- Yes, he was fine, but I could have visited him more often.

Psychologist:

- It's also important to remember that you live in different states. You have your own life, family, and job, which means you're very busy. To visit him, you usually need a long holiday or vacation.

Amanda:

- Yes, that's true.

Psychologist:

- I'd like you to write down everything we discussed today. Reflect on these points and consider the possibility of visiting your mother. It will likely be good for both you and her.

Amanda:

- Okay, I'll think about it and talk to my boss to see if I can get a few days off to visit my mother.

The following week, Amanda managed to get some time off from work and traveled to see her mother. Their reunion was emotional since they hadn't seen each other in many months. They cried a lot, and Amanda apologized for not visiting sooner, but her mother understood because it was very painful for both of them.

Amanda began to revisit the rooms of the house where she had grown up, filled with so many memories. She and her mother looked at old photos of her father smiling and playing with them. This was very important for Amanda's process of overcoming and accepting her grief.

One reason Amanda struggled to accept the situation, besides guilt, was her fear of how her mother was coping. However, her mother had gone through the grieving process more quickly. While she still thought of her late husband, as memories never truly fade, she was no longer suffering.

Amanda's mother had donated most of her husband's clothes and made some changes to the house. At first, this made Amanda feel a bit uncomfortable, but she gradually realized it was important because her mother needed to move on.

After talking a lot with her mother, Amanda's feeling of guilt started to dissipate. Being in the house and seeing that her father was really no longer there helped her come to terms with reality. Although she knew rationally that he was gone, she was now beginning to understand it emotionally. She did the exercises her psychologist had given her, which also made her feel more relieved.

While still at her mother's house, Amanda had an online session with her psychologist and shared how the reunion went and how she was feeling.

Amanda:

- I'm feeling more relieved. It now seems like I'm really starting to understand that he's gone. At first, it was very difficult, but seeing that my mother was doing well was a great relief. I thought I had to stay in mourning for my father's memory, that I couldn't forget him because he was such a wonderful father. But I've realized that accepting the grief doesn't mean I'll forget him. I'll keep the precious memories I have with him while understanding and accepting that he has truly gone.

Psychologist:

- That's very good. You're moving into the fifth stage of grief, which is acceptance. This means you're recognizing that it's a situation you can't change, but at the same time, you don't need to stop living your life because of your father's loss.

Now I'm going to give you an exercise you can do to "say goodbye" to him. It's called the closure letter, where you can write everything you would have liked to say to him, expressing your feelings and saying goodbye.

Closure Letter
Dear Dad, First of all, I want to thank you for all the years we spent together, for all the lessons learned, and all the laughter. Thank you for always being there with me through the good times and the bad, always

giving me advice and guidance. Whether it was when I struggled with school subjects, you would sit with me and say it was normal not to understand some math problems or forget some history dates, and that I was very intelligent and clever and would go far.

When I had romantic disappointments, you always consoled me and helped me see that while my feelings were important and I needed to experience them to gain wisdom, I would someday meet someone special—and that indeed happened. I remember you walking me down the aisle on my wedding day, telling me everything had worked out. Your guidance on raising my children was invaluable.

I want to ask for your forgiveness, for even though I might not have been the perfect daughter, I will never forget all the wonderful moments we shared—our outings and trips together. Most importantly, I want to tell you that I love you and will never forget you.

This was the final step for Amanda to fully enter the fifth stage of grief, which is the acceptance process. After this, she continued to think of her father, remembering him, but this time not with sorrow, but with joy for the incredible person he was.

The closure letter is a technique that can be used in various situations such as deaths, relationship endings, relocations, etc. It allows you to consciously bring closure to that situation and helps you start moving forward. If needed, read the letter for several days until you feel a sense of closure.

After Amanda completed this technique, she finally accepted her father's passing and could resume her life in a lighter manner, without being hindered.

Chapter XII
Memory, Focus e Concentration

Luiz (fictional name), aged 39, arrived at the psychologist's office with specific complaints. He had been experiencing forgetfulness, often couldn't recall where he put his keys, sometimes forgot things people told him, and frequently lost track of appointments unless reminded by his wife.

He started to worry, scheduling multiple doctor's visits and undergoing various tests because he suspected a neurological problem. However, medical examinations showed no abnormalities. Why then was he facing these memory and concentration difficulties?

There are several possibilities when someone complains of memory and concentration problems. Initially, it's crucial to rule out any neurological changes, brain diseases, or impairments. If none of these are identified, there are other avenues to explore.

Today, something that is often considered, especially when these symptoms arise, is the well-known Attention-Deficit/Hyperactivity Disorder (ADHD). The issue is, if you search for symptoms online, it's likely you'll identify with most or all of them, but that doesn't necessarily mean you actually have ADHD. To confirm whether you have this disorder, it's essential to consult a specialist—a psychologist, neuropsychologist, or psychiatrist. Through these professionals, you'll undergo tests and scales that diagnose whether

ADHD is present and to what extent. Depending on the severity, you may require medication and psychological support.

Below, I'll explain a bit about ADHD, but please note that this is purely informative. For a diagnosis, you should seek out a specialized professional.

Attention-Deficit/Hyperactivity Disorder (ADHD) is a neuropsychiatric disorder that typically manifests in childhood but can persist into adolescence and adulthood. Symptoms of ADHD can vary in intensity and include difficulties with attention, hyperactivity, and impulsivity. Here are some of the most common symptoms of ADHD:

Difficulty in Attention:

- Difficulty paying attention to details or making careless mistakes in schoolwork, at work, or in other activities.
- Trouble maintaining focus on tasks or activities, especially those that are lengthy or tedious.
- Seems not to listen when directly addressed.
- Difficulty following instructions or completing tasks.

Hyperactivity:

- Excessive restlessness, such as being unable to stay seated in situations where it's expected, like at school or work.
- Constantly moving hands or feet, fidgeting, or being unable to remain still.
- Difficulty playing or engaging in leisure activities quietly.

Impulsivity:

- Difficulty waiting for their turn in lines or group situations.
- Frequently interrupts others or intrudes on conversations or games.
- Trouble controlling emotional reactions, like anger or frustration.

It's important to note that ADHD symptoms can vary from person to person and may manifest differently at different stages of life. Some individuals with ADHD may predominantly display symptoms of inattention, while others may predominantly exhibit symptoms of hyperactivity and impulsivity.

In some cases, ADHD symptoms can significantly impair a person's social, academic, or occupational functioning.

Psychologist:

Before we delve into memory itself, we need to
consider information retention. For instance,
nowadays people tend to live on autopilot. Imagine
you're driving to work — has it ever happened that
you arrive at work and can't remember the route
you took?

Luiz:

- Many times, sometimes I don't even remember
what was on the way to work. There were times
when I arrived at work and my wife messaged me
asking if I noticed whether a store was open, and I
told her I didn't even pay attention to that store.
There were also times when I parked the car on the
street and later couldn't remember where I had left
it.

Psychologist:

- This directly relates to issues of attention because
if you didn't pay attention to something, how is
your brain supposed to retrieve that information if
it wasn't encoded in the first place?

Most of the time, this is exactly what happens. For
example, if your boss asks for a report to be
delivered by Wednesday at 10:00 AM, but you
were distracted thinking about other things, there's

a good chance that by Wednesday you haven't
completed that report because your brain didn't
encode that information.

Psychologist:

Our brain also tends to discard what isn't as
relevant and sets aside certain information. For
example, imagine you're extremely anxious about
an important meeting at work. You're solely
focused on this situation and end up not paying
attention to where you parked your car or if you set
the alarm. Later in the day, you might worry about
whether you set the alarm and perhaps have to
return to your car to check during lunchtime, or you
might try to remember on which street you parked
and struggle to recall. This doesn't necessarily
mean there's something wrong with your brain;
rather, that information became less important
compared to the meeting you were very anxious
about.

Luiz:

Wow, that's a relief. I thought something was
wrong with me. But how can I improve my focus
and memory?

Psychologist:

There are several important points for us to work
on:

Our brain is not a machine: Many people liken our brain to a supercomputer capable of storing vast amounts of information. While this isn't entirely wrong, relying solely on this notion can be detrimental. Our memory and concentration are influenced by various factors such as age, stress, and mental stimulation. The more you challenge your brain, the stronger it becomes. However, it's essential to use auxiliary tools to support your brain. Try taking notes of things you need to remember, use a digital or physical planner, as there's a high chance of forgetting things otherwise.

Factors that impair attention and memory: Poor sleep quality—whether due to difficulty falling asleep, inadequate sleep duration, or frequent awakenings—can impair attention and memory. When the brain isn't fully alert, it craves rest, reducing energy levels. Therefore, practicing Sleep Hygiene techniques is crucial (Chapter V).

Practice Mindfulness and Meditation: Mindfulness and meditation are excellent techniques for enhancing focus and concentration. They encourage being present in the moment, focusing on current activities and sensations. Set aside time each day to practice these techniques, particularly during automatic routines. For example, if you commute to work by car, try taking a different route and focus on the surroundings—notice shops, houses, and other vehicles—to enhance presence. This will benefit various aspects of your life.

Exercise your brain: Think of exercising your brain like starting a physical workout routine at the gym. Initially, you might lift light weights, say 1kg. As you continue exercising, you get stronger and progress to heavier weights like 2kg, 3kg, and so forth.

Similarly, if you're someone who operates on autopilot or mentally inactive, your brain may become 'flabby' and struggle to 'carry heavy loads'. However, by consistently exercising your brain, it becomes stronger and can retain more information, improving attention and memory.

Look for games and apps that stimulate memory, engage in activities with your non-dominant hand like writing, brushing your teeth, try to exercise your memory, challenge yourself to remember specific things from day to day, such as what did I eat for lunch? What did I eat yesterday? What did I eat three days ago? It may seem trivial, but many people can't even recall what they ate for breakfast or lunch because they lack this practice and don't pay attention to what they're doing, so break out of autopilot.

Chapter XIII
Coping with Depression

Depression is becoming increasingly prevalent in our society, along with various other issues previously addressed such as stress and anxiety. Unfortunately, many people still consider depression to be nonsense, something trivial, and there is still significant stigma surrounding it today.

Statements like:
"This is lack of God"
"It's just boredom"
"I'll give you a pile of dishes to wash"
"There are people in much worse situations than yours"
"He's loaded, has a car, house, family, what depression?"

Unfortunately, these are still very common in everyday life, whether with ordinary people or celebrities. Depression does not discriminate based on gender, race, or social class; it can affect anyone.

There are many causes for depression; it can be genetic, meaning if a mother or family members have depression, their children are more likely to develop it. It can also be caused by trauma, significant stress factors, or losses. Depression has multiple causes, but it's important to remember that there are treatments available. Some cases require medication along with therapy, while others can be managed through therapy and other practices.

It is important to remember that there are differences between depression and occasional sad or low days.

Differentiating between momentary sadness and depression can be challenging, as both can involve feelings of sadness and discouragement. However, there are important distinctions between them that can help distinguish between fleeting sadness and a depressive episode:

Duration and Persistence: Transient sadness is usually temporary and may be triggered by specific events such as disappointment, loss, or setbacks. It tends to diminish over time as the person adapts to the situation or finds ways to cope. In contrast, depression is a persistent and chronic condition that can last for weeks, months, or even years, significantly affecting a person's daily functioning.

Intensity of Symptoms: While fleeting sadness can be intense and cause emotional discomfort, symptoms of depression are generally more severe and debilitating. This may include profound feelings of hopelessness, helplessness, and emptiness, as well as a significant loss of interest or pleasure in activities that were once enjoyed.

Impact on Daily Activities: Transient sadness may temporarily interfere with a person's daily activities, but it generally does not completely impair their ability to function. On the other hand, depression can significantly impair performance at work, in studies, in relationships, and in other areas of life, making it difficult to even perform simple daily tasks.

Presence of Other Symptoms: In addition to persistent sadness, depression may be associated with a range of other symptoms such as changes in appetite or weight, sleep difficulties, fatigue, low self-esteem, difficulty concentrating, feelings of guilt or worthlessness, agitation or psychomotor retardation, and thoughts of death or suicide.

Response to Positive Events: While a person experiencing transient sadness may temporarily feel discouraged even in the face of positive events, someone with depression may struggle to experience joy or pleasure, even in situations that would normally be gratifying.

Ana (fictional name), 39 years old, has had severe depression diagnosed since she was 25 years old and has been undergoing medication treatment since then. Initially, people dismissed her depression as trivial, but over time they began to understand the seriousness of the situation.

She had periods in her life, especially before the diagnosis, when she couldn't get out of bed for days, didn't shower, neglected everyday activities, and needed to be practically carried by her family to do anything. She didn't work or study; her life was stagnant. After the diagnosis and starting to take medications prescribed by a psychiatrist, she improved significantly. She began to feel more motivated, secured a job, started studying, but she lacked stability. She would start therapy and then stop; there were times she even stopped taking medication on her own, which led to a rebound effect, making her feel worse than before taking the medication.

After much suffering, she decided to seek therapy and commit to the sessions because she realized she couldn't continue alone, despite support and medication. During her first session with the psychologist, she recounted her entire history, and it became clear she needed to take a new direction in her life. For this reason, she started working with the psychologist on emotional regulation techniques (Chapter V), Wheel of Life (Chapter II), and needed to work on her worldview through thought recording (Chapter VII). Various techniques and strategies were used so that she could sustain herself and live her life in a lighter and healthier way.

The problem was that sometimes she struggled to complete tasks, had difficulty starting what needed to be done. When she managed to start, she performed well, but during phases when she couldn't get out of bed, this was very challenging.

For this reason, the psychologist decided to work with something different and very important when dealing with depression:

Behavioral Activation

Behavioral activation is an excellent practice for treating depression because it focuses on helping individuals engage in meaningful and pleasurable activities as a way to combat depression and improve mood and overall well-being.

A very important first step is to start with simple activities that the person can do without much effort, such as making the bed. It may seem like a small task, but many people with depression struggle to complete it. When you begin with making the bed, it's like telling your body that there's no need to stay lying down—it's a first step to start your day. In addition to this, there are other important practices that can be done, such as:

Identification of Meaningful Activities: It's important to try to identify activities that are important, meaningful, or enjoyable to you. This can include hobbies, interests, social activities, work or family responsibilities, physical exercise, among others.

Activity Planning: Once meaningful activities have been identified, you can create a structured activity plan. This may involve setting realistic and specific goals related to the activities, as well as creating a schedule to accomplish them.

Gradual Activity Increase: Behavioral activation focuses on gradually increasing activity over time. This may involve identifying initially simple or small activities that you can successfully complete and gradually expanding to more challenging or demanding activities.

Activity Monitoring and Records: It's important to keep a record of activities completed, including the type of activity, duration, level of pleasure or satisfaction, and any associated thoughts or emotions. This helps you identify patterns and make adjustments as needed.

Identifying and Addressing Barriers: It's also important to identify any barriers that may be preventing engagement in meaningful activities, such as negative thoughts, limiting beliefs, or practical difficulties. Then, develop strategies to effectively address these barriers.

Positive Reinforcement: Behavioral activation emphasizes the use of positive reinforcement to encourage and reward engagement in meaningful activities. This may involve recognizing successes, celebrating achievements, and providing ongoing encouragement from yourself, close ones, and the psychologist.

This was a very important step for Ana to handle daily situations in a healthier way. Even on days when she felt more depressed, she managed not to be paralyzed and was able to carry out daily activities, albeit in a gentler manner, without forcing herself to be extremely productive.

In addition to these issues, another very important point was working on acceptance of situations—not passive acceptance in the sense of doing nothing to change them, but Ana needed to understand that it's natural to have good days where she can accomplish more activities and other days that are more challenging.

She often had a cycle of self-criticism, so when she planned to do something and couldn't at times, it generated feelings of frustration and anger for not being able to do what she had set out to do. However, she began to understand that there are situations beyond her control, and sometimes it's difficult to do what she would like due to emotions. She started to accept that these moments could happen, but at the same time, she understood that even if this happened, she could try to perform necessary activities in a gentler manner so as not to be completely stagnant.

Through these practices, she began to live life more lightly, even though she understood that depression was not curable. She learned to cope with depression without letting it be debilitating.

Chapter XIV

Healthy or Toxic relationship?

Nowadays it seems increasingly difficult to have healthy relationships, which is why the demand for couples therapy has been increasing significantly. This is a good sign because it indicates that people want to improve their relationships and not give up easily. Many people complain about issues their partners have some don't communicate enough, others talk too much about each other's behaviors, and the difficulty of dealing with one another. There are many aspects that can harm relationships, and we need to identify what we are doing that can either improve or harm our daily coexistence.

I want to start by pointing out what unhealthy relationships are, because there are various aspects that can be very harmful to those who experience this type of relationship.

Toxic Relationship

A very common term nowadays seen on social media, videos, and even discussed by many experts is the famous toxic relationship, but how do you identify if you're in one?

A toxic relationship is a type where the behaviors of one or both partners are emotionally or physically harmful to the other. These relationships are characterized by dynamics that erode self-esteem, trust, and emotional well-being of those involved. Some common characteristics of a toxic relationship include:

Control and Manipulation: One partner tries to control or manipulate the other, whether through possessive behavior, excessive jealousy, or attempts to isolate the other from friends and family.

Lack of Respect: There's a lack of respect where one partner devalues or belittles the other. This can manifest through constant criticism, insults, or derogatory remarks.

Destructive Communication: Communication is dominated by frequent fights, accusations, or a passive-aggressive tone. Conflict resolution is rare, and problems are often ignored or escalated.

Emotional or Physical Abuse: There may be emotional abuse, such as gaslighting, emotional blackmail, or physical abuse involving violence or threats of violence.

Power Imbalance: One partner may have disproportionate control over important decisions, finances, or other aspects of the shared life, leaving the other voiceless or lacking autonomy.

Lack of Support: In a toxic relationship, partners do not support each other in their interests and needs. One partner may devalue or discourage the other's dreams and aspirations.

Emotional Instability: The relationship may be marked by intense highs and lows, with moments of intense passion followed by fights or emotional crises, which can also be a form of manipulation.

Constant Mistrust: There's a lack of trust where one or both partners constantly suspect betrayals or lies, regardless of concrete evidence.

Emotional Neglect: One partner may be emotionally unavailable or neglectful, failing to offer necessary support or emotional connection.

Identifying these signs is crucial to recognizing and addressing a toxic relationship, as they can severely impact mental health and overall well-being.

Being in a toxic relationship can have serious negative effects on mental and emotional health, leading to feelings of anxiety, depression, and low self-esteem. Recognizing these dynamics is the first step towards seeking help, whether through counseling, therapy, or, in many cases, the decision to leave the relationship to preserve personal well-being.

Emotional Dependence

Emotional dependence is a psychological state in which a person excessively relies on another to fulfill their emotional needs, such as self-esteem, security, and happiness. This dependency can occur in various types of relationships, including romantic, familial, or friendships.

There are several characteristics of Emotional Dependence that are crucial to identify:

Fear of Loneliness: The person experiences intense fear of being alone and feels a constant need to be in the company of others, even if the relationship is harmful.

Continuous Approval Seeking: The emotionally dependent individual constantly seeks approval and validation from others to feel valued and confident. Their decisions and actions are often influenced by the desire to please or avoid disapproval.

Excessive Sacrifice: To maintain the relationship, the emotionally dependent person may sacrifice their own needs, desires, and interests, often placing the well-being of the other above their own.

Low Self-Esteem: The person often has a negative self-image and low self-esteem, believing they cannot be happy or complete without the other.

Difficulty Making Decisions Alone: The emotionally dependent person struggles to make decisions without consulting their partner or seeking their approval, feeling insecure about their own judgment.

Jealousy and Insecurity: The individual may experience extreme jealousy and insecurity, constantly fearing abandonment or that their partner does not love them as much as they desire.

Constant Need for Reassurance: There is a continual need for reassurance of love and commitment from the partner, leading to behaviors such as seeking constant guarantees and promises of love.

Emotional dependence can lead to various harms such as:

Loss of Identity: The emotionally dependent person may lose their sense of identity as their needs and desires are often suppressed to please others.

Anxiety and Depression: The constant need for approval and fear of abandonment can result in high levels of anxiety and depression.

Overcoming emotional dependence involves a process of self-discovery and strengthening self-esteem.

Developing Self-Esteem: Working to improve self-esteem by recognizing and appreciating your own qualities and abilities. An excellent tool to enhance self-esteem is to make a list of qualities and achievements you have had throughout your life. It's common to forget or overlook your strengths, even if they seem simple. Continuously reinforce what you like and what you do well in yourself.

Building Autonomy: Practicing independent decision-making and engaging in activities that provide personal satisfaction and fulfillment.

Establishing Healthy Boundaries: Learning to establish and maintain healthy boundaries in relationships, ensuring that your own needs and desires are respected.

Building a Support Network: Cultivating friendships and relationships outside of the primary relationship, ensuring a diverse support network.

Recognizing emotional dependence is the first step toward a healthier and more balanced emotional life, allowing for relationships based on mutual respect and autonomy.

Healthy Relationship

A healthy relationship is characterized by mutual respect, open communication, emotional support, and a balance between the needs and desires of both partners. These relationships promote the well-being of those involved and are essential for a satisfying and balanced emotional life.

Some of the key characteristics and necessary elements for a healthy relationship include:

Mutual Respect: Both partners respect and value each other's opinions, feelings, and boundaries. There is no room for devaluation or belittlement.

Open Communication: Communication is honest, open, and frequent. Partners feel comfortable expressing their concerns, feelings, and desires without fear of judgment or retaliation, and they do not ignore each other for days.

Trust: There is a deep level of trust between partners. They trust each other and avoid behaviors that could undermine that trust, such as lying or betrayals.

Emotional Support: Partners emotionally support each other, being present in times of difficulty and celebrating each other's achievements.

Independence and Autonomy: While it is important to be together and engage in joint activities, each partner maintains their own identity and independence. They have interests and activities outside of the relationship, which are encouraged and respected.

Equality: The relationship is balanced, with both partners contributing equally to the relationship and playing an active role in important decisions.

Healthy Conflict Resolution: When conflicts arise, they are addressed constructively. Partners approach problems calmly and seek solutions that are acceptable to both.

Affection and Care: There are regular demonstrations of affection and care, both physical and emotional, which strengthen the connection between partners.

Some ways to have and maintain a healthy relationship involve:

Self-awareness: Knowing yourself, including your needs, desires, and limits, is fundamental to entering a relationship in a healthy way. This helps in clearly communicating your expectations to your partner.

Empathy: Being able to understand and share your partner's feelings is crucial for building a deep and meaningful connection.

Commitment: Both partners must be committed to working on the relationship and growing together, facing challenges collaboratively.

Quality Time: Spending quality time together, engaging in activities both enjoy, strengthens the emotional bond and creates positive memories.

Mutual Trust: Building and maintaining trust is essential. This involves being honest, reliable, and consistent in your actions.

Flexibility: Being flexible and willing to adapt to changes and the needs of your partner is important for the longevity and health of the relationship.

Intimacy: Maintaining emotional and physical intimacy is important. This can include deep conversations, sharing feelings and experiences, and maintaining a satisfying sexual life.

Reciprocal Support: Supporting each other's personal and professional growth, encouraging each other's goals and dreams, strengthens the partnership.

To maintain a healthy relationship, it's important to communicate regularly and effectively. Make time to discuss the relationship, share feelings, and resolve issues before they escalate. Remember to regularly show gratitude and appreciation for your partner, as this helps maintain a positive atmosphere in the relationship. It's important to resolve conflicts constructively, addressing them calmly without personal attacks, and focusing on solving the problem rather than blaming each other. Encourage and respect each other's individuality, allowing space for personal activities and interests. A healthy relationship is built on mutual respect, clear and open communication, and a continuous commitment from both partners to grow and improve together.

Chapter XV

What are the 10 percent?

As I mentioned at the beginning of the book and in the title itself, the idea is that with these techniques, tools, and experiences, you can solve 90% of your problems. It would be impossible for me to promise to solve 100% of your problems because there are very specific issues that are unique to each person. There are physical and mental illnesses that go beyond what can be resolved through techniques and tools presented in a book. You may be experiencing such great suffering that even with this book, you may need professional assistance, for example.

Let's imagine that you have a family member going through a very specific case, such as Alzheimer's, Schizophrenia; I would like to help, but unfortunately, my book will not directly assist you with these issues.

However, this does not mean that even in specific situations, you cannot benefit from the techniques and tools presented in this book. For example, imagine you are facing severe financial difficulties. Unfortunately, this book does not have the lottery numbers to pay your bills and help family and friends. However, you can use the problem-solving technique (Chapter VIII) to try to find ways to improve your financial situation.

If you or a family member is experiencing a physical illness, you can use the thought record (Chapter VII) to analyze the situation, try to find a different way to view and even cope with what is keeping you awake.

Even if I haven't mentioned a particular illness or specific issue in this book, try to reflect on what has been discussed here, on the techniques and tools, and try to adapt them as much as possible to your reality, to the problem you are facing.

In other words, even if you can't directly solve these 10% of the problems, you can still find ways to live a lighter life.

I hope you have enjoyed this book and that it can help you find solutions to your problems and provide quality of life and well-being for you, your family, and loved ones. And once again, remember, if you are experiencing great suffering, seek help from a psychologist, psychiatrist, or another healthcare professional.

References

BECK, Judith S. Terapia cognitivo-comportamental: Teoria e prática. 3. ed. Porto Alegre: Artmed, 2021. 432 p.

WILLIAMS, Mark; PENMAN, Danny. Atenção plena (Mindfulness): Como Encontrar a paz em um mundo frenético. São Paulo: Sextante, 2023. 208 p.

SOUZA, Henrique Santos. Micropassos: Guia prático. São Paulo: Sinopsys Editora e Sistemas LTDA ME, 2024. 96 p.

WRIGHT, Jesse H.; BROWN, Gregory K.; THASE, Michael E.; BASCO, Monica R. Aprendendo a terapia cognitivo-comportamental: Um guia ilustrado. Porto Alegre: Artmed, 2018. 256 p.

FALCO, Diego. Essencial da Terapia Cognitivo-Comportamental: TCC para Iniciantes e Estudantes. [Recurso eletrônico]. São Paulo, 2019. E-book. 256 p.

Carroll, Lewis. Alice no País das Maravilhas (Classic Edition). Editora Darkside, 2019. 224 p.

BARKLEY, Russell A.; BENTON, Christine M.; PICON, Felipe Almeida. Vencendo o TDAH Adulto: Transtorno de Déficit de Atenção/Hiperatividade. Tradução de Felipe

Almeida Picon. 1. ed. Porto Alegre: Artmed, 2022. 300 p.

LEAHY, Robert L.; OLIVEIRA, Irismar Reis de (Trad.). Técnicas de Terapia Cognitiva: Manual do Terapeuta. 1. ed. Porto Alegre: Artmed, 2018. 536 p.

GREENBERGER, Dennis; PADESKY, Christine A.; RANGÉ, Bernard (Trad.). A Mente Vencendo o Humor: Mude como Você se Sente, Mudando o Modo como Você Pensa. 2. ed. Porto Alegre: Artmed, 2016. 352 p.